T0146415

A Biblical Theology Behind

Music, Praise, and Worship

DR. MARK PEARCE

authorHOUSE®

AuthorHouse™ UK
1663 Liberty Drive
Bloomington, IN 47403 USA
www.authorhouse.co.uk
Phone: 0800.197.4150

Published by AuthorHouse 01/16/2018

ISBN: 978-1-5246-7727-5 (sc)
ISBN: 978-1-5246-7728-2 (hc)
ISBN: 978-1-5246-7726-8 (e)

I dedicate this book to my mom and dad, Frank and Alvita Pearce. We will always love you, and you will both always be in our memories.

Contents

Acknowledgements

I would like to give my sincere gratitude to the following people.

To my wife, Deborah, thank you for always being by my side. You have been a tower of strength to me. Your ministry is awesome. God has called you and ordained you even before you were conceived in your mother's womb (Jeremiah 1: 5). You have the strength of your namesake, Deborah (Judges 4: 9–10), the faithfulness of Ruth (Ruth 1: 16–17), and the courage of Esther (Esther 4: 15–16). I thank God for you, my love. You are my faithful friend and lover, Ani ohev otach.

I want to say how proud I am of our son, Matthew, and our daughter, Elisha. The joy that you have both brought into my life is immeasurable. Thank you both for your encouragement and prayers, I love you both, with all my heart. God bless you xx.

Thanks to Julie Porter, a close friend and colleague. Julie, you are a very special friend of my family. You have been there for us to encourage us, pray with us, and cry with us, and you have stood with us through good and bad times. Also, thank you for the times when you were not timid to correct us; you are truly a friend (Proverbs 27: 17). Thank you for your advice and assistance in refining this book; words cannot express my appreciation. Your contribution is incalculable. God bless!

Most importantly, I give all praise and thanks to Yahweh, the most high God, who is my foundation and my all. He has been my inspiration and has led me throughout the whole process of writing this book. Without Him, I would not have been able to accomplish this final work. I give all praise and thanks to my Heavenly Father.

Let a man so consider us, as servants of Christ and stewards of
the mysteries of God. Moreover it is required in stewards that
one be found faithful. But with me it is a very small thing that I
should be judged by you or by a human court. In fact, I do not
even judge myself. For I know of nothing against myself, yet I
am not justified by this; but He who judges me is the Lord.

Therefore judge nothing before the time, until the Lord comes, who
will both bring to light the hidden things of darkness and reveal the
counsels of the hearts. Then each one's praise will come from God.

1 Corinthians 4: 1–5

Chapter 1

Music from a Biblical Perspective – Lucifer and Subliminal Messages

Jubal and Biblical Music History

There are many non-biblical mythological theories and thoughts concerning the true beginning of music. However, according to Moses and recorded in the first book of the Torah (the first five books of the Old Testament), a man by the name of Jubal was the father of all those who played the harp and organ (Genesis 4: 21).

The period during which Jubal began to develop musical instruments is unknown. However, some theologians say that he developed the כנור kinnor, also known as the harp, from which all stringed instruments derived, and the עוגב ugab, also known as the organ, from which all wind instruments derived, nearly 1,500 years before the flood during Noah's time.

However, the organ must not be confused with the traditional instrument found in the modern-day church. In fact, it was a woodwind instrument (to be explained in more detail later in this chapter). However, unbelievable to some, the origins of music entering the earthly realm can be argued to go back even further than Jubal. Some theologians believe it was Lucifer himself who became the portal for the origins of music.

So, as there seem to be arguments that the origin of music dates back to possibly within 160 years of humans on earth, I feel it wise to focus my research on the biblical perspective of the origins of music. I want to further investigate and present my research findings on the theory that music actually began when God placed it within Lucifer. This research may not be accepted by some theological circles, but it has a valid place in the argument of the origins of music.

As we read the Bible, we see it is permeated with account upon account of the use and enjoyment of music. Why is this? In a time before modern television, concerts, and electric musical instruments, music was an integral part of life, particularly in Old Testament times. In fact, if we could step back into this time, we would see biblical accounts come to life. For example, we would see women playing the timbrel (called the toph) or masses of people blowing rams' horns (known as the shofar) while singing and dancing. Additionally, music would have been heard coming from the temple as people were gathering or in the act of worship. Such was the influence of music in this period as they worshipped Yahweh.

Incidentally, Yahweh is God's personal name (Exodus 3: 15). In the Bible, LORD, written all in capitals, represents YHWH. In Hebrew, God's name is written using the letters yod, hey, vav, hey. In English, the transliteration is Y-H-W-H. It is important to say here that the Hebrew language does not contain any vowels. When transcribed, the tetragrammaton YHWH is often pronounced Yahweh or Jehovah. However, I personally prefer Yahweh, and from here on, I may interchange the words 'Yahweh' and 'God', but He is the same Creator of the universe.

Yahweh means the One who exists. Its root word is actually hayah, which translates in English as 'I am'. Interestingly, 'I Am that I Am' (Exodus 3: 14), which is transliterated as 'hayah asher hayah,' also means the existing One. Furthermore, Jesus made the declaration of 'I Am' on numerous occasions, one of which is in the account of John 8: 37–59, the key verse being verse 58: 'Jesus said to them, "Most assuredly, I say to you, before Abraham was, I AM."'

Origins of Lucifer

This section explains the origins of Lucifer, his proper name, and finally, what this being is.

It is a widely accepted theological stance that whilst in heaven, Lucifer was the chief worship leader. However, is this stance truly correct, and if so, how does this affect the act of humankind's worship to God? It is recorded in the Bible that the two major prophets, Ezekiel and Isaiah, describe a heavenly conversation concerning Lucifer. Firstly, we analyse the words of Ezekiel recorded in the book of Ezekiel 28: 13–15.

> You were in Eden, the garden of God; Every precious stone was your covering: The sardius, topaz, and diamond, Beryl, onyx, and jasper, Sapphire, turquoise, and emerald with gold. The workmanship of your timbrels and pipes was prepared for you on the day you were created. You were the anointed cherub who covers; I established you; You were on the holy mountain of God; You walked back and forth in the midst of fiery stones. You were perfect in your ways

> from the day you were created, Till iniquity was
> found in you.

Notice that Ezekiel states that Lucifer was created by God with tabrets and pipes in him. Before we go any further, we must explain what is meant by tabrets and pipes.

'Tabret' is the Hebrew word תֹּף 'toph', meaning 'tambourine'. 'Pipe' is the Hebrew word נֶקֶב 'neqeb', meaning to bore through. Could neqeb be linked to an instrument similar to a flute in modern-day terms? If so, it can be argued that Ezekiel is actually stating that Yahweh created musical instruments and placed them within His creation. Based on this summary, many theologians believe Yahweh created Lucifer this way to lead praise and worship in heaven. All other heavenly beings are described as worshippers around the throne of God or as angels sent out to do God's divine bidding. Lucifer is the only one described as being created with musical instruments within him. This cannot be a coincidence; the instruments built within him were established by the Creator of all things.

God has a purpose and a plan for everything He does. As such, I argue that it can be concluded that the instruments placed within Lucifer were there for no other reason but that of playing music and worshipping God.

At this point, it is beneficial to further discover who or what is this musical being Lucifer. Firstly, let's discuss his name. The name 'Lucifer' is translated from the original Hebrew word הֵילֵל – 'Heylel' – found in Isaiah 14: 12. It means shining one, light bearer, day star, morning star. So why Lucifer and not Heylel? Let me explain. Although Heylel is the original word, it is imperative to note that Jesus Christ is also referred to in the Scriptures as the day star (2 Peter 1: 19) and the bright and morning star (Revelation 22: 16). There can be some confusion as to why Jesus and Lucifer are both called the day star or morning star. Let me attempt to bring some clarification to this seemingly confusing issue.

There are various translations of the Hebrew text. Two of the most popular are the Latin Vulgate and the Greek Septuagint. When we look at the original Hebrew word 'Heylel' in Isaiah 14: 12, it is translated in the Latin Vulgate as phosphoros and in the Septuagint as heosphoros. Both words translate as daystar. The Latin translation of heosphoros is Lucifer. Hence, the word 'Lucifer' is used in some Bible versions to avoid confusion between Jesus and Lucifer. Some modern-day versions of the Bible have the name 'day star' or 'morning star' for the word 'Lucifer'. Personally, I feel Lucifer is an accurate translation, but you must keep in mind that the original name is Heylel. So do not be confused if I interchange Lucifer and Heylel; they are the same being.

Let me give you an example. A parent names his or her child Peter in the English tongue and with the English spelling. However, a Spanish translation of that name is Pedro. In the English language, Pedro sounds and looks different, but it means the same thing. Only the parents will know the true original pronunciation and the reason they named their child Peter. In the same vein, God created and gave the name Heylel.

Heylel was an angel in heaven, and his beauty was magnified by the fact that every precious stone covered him. But they and the musical instruments placed within him were there to reflect God's glory and not to draw attention to himself.

Here it is significant to highlight the fact that the precious stones that God placed within Heylel can only reflect natural light when faceted or cut at certain degrees in order to capture and reflect that light. A professional cutter knows how many cuts to make and where to make them to capture and reflect the light, thereby creating the sparkle. Hence, even though Heylel was the light bearer, without God, who is the light of the world (2 Samuel 22: 29 and John 8: 12), the light cannot be emitted.

Further, the word 'Heylel' derives from the same root as the Hebrew word 'halal', which is the root word of 'hallelu', which means 'to praise'. Thus, the universal word 'Hallelujah' means 'Praise Yah' or, more specifically, 'praise Yahweh'. So Heylel, deriving from the word 'hallelujah', is another reason why theologians believe he was created to lead praise unto Yahweh in the heavenly realm.

Ezekiel states that God placed Heylel on His holy mountain and that Heylel was able to 'walk up and down in the midst of the stones of fire' (Ezekiel 28: 14). In Adam Clarke's Commentary on the Bible, he deduces that this statement means that Heylel's path was paved with precious stones that shone and sparkled like fire. God had created Heylel perfect; problems arose only when 'iniquity was found in him' (Ezekiel 28: 15). This became Heylel's downfall.

Isaiah states that Heylel's downfall was due to his pomp. The word 'pomp' is the Hebrew word 'ga'own', meaning 'pride' and 'arrogance'. As such, Heylel's pride was the main factor that led to his downfall.

> Your pomp is brought down to Sheol, And the sound
> of your stringed instruments; The maggot is spread
> under you, And worms cover you.' "How you are
> fallen from heaven, O Lucifer, son of the morning!
> How you are cut down to the ground,

You who weakened the nations! For you have said in your heart: 'I will ascend into heaven, I will exalt my throne above the stars of God; I will also sit on the mount of the congregation on the farthest sides of the north; I will ascend above the heights of the clouds, I will be like the Most High.' Yet you shall be brought down to Sheol, To the lowest depths of the Pit. (Isaiah 14: 11–15)

Isaiah states that Heylel was expelled from heaven; this is confirmed centuries later by John the Divine in Revelation 12: 9. More importantly, Jesus Himself described the scene saying, 'I saw Satan fall like lightning from heaven.' (Luke 10: 18). He no longer held the position of the bearer of God's light; he now became the very enemy of God and subsequently God's people, often trying to mask himself as an angel of light to deceive mankind! (2 Corinthians 11: 14) It is imperative to keep at the forefront of our minds that whilst he was in heaven, he had a name that glorified God. However, after his fall, his name changed from Heylel, meaning shining one, light bearer, day star, morning star, to Satan, meaning enemy or adversary. He also has various epithets, some of which are deceiver, devil, and the accuser of the saints. Remember, even Jesus called him Satan.

Subliminal Messages

Although not to be discussed here in length, subliminal messages within music are messages placed just below the human hearing threshold passed to the human mind without the mind being consciously aware of it. This is done to convey a secret message into the psyche of the listener. It can also be achieved by using certain music styles and songs to manipulate the listener to feel a certain way. Record and advertising companies pay great deals of money to use this method. Hence it is imperative that the Christian is vigilant to what he or she is listening to and to seek God for His help in eradicating any unwanted influence.

Such is Satan's strong association with the origins of music that George Whitefield, Anglican Protestant minister (1714 to 1770) asked why the devil should have all the best tunes, a viewpoint echoed by some modern day Christians. It is a well-documented rationale amongst some Christians that non-Christian music is evil and should not be listened to by Christians. Music genres such as Christian rock, Christian hip-hop, Christian thrash metal, Christian pop music, and the list goes on, are frowned upon and seen as an avenue of compromising God's word in order to make Christianity fashionable for young people. Is there any truth in these concerns? After all, music belongs to God. The devil has no ownership on it, does he? Should we not be all things to all people (1 Corinthians 9: 22–23) and use any tool available to us to evangelise God's word?

To answer these questions, one must look carefully at Isaiah's words. He states that Satan was expelled from heaven and brought down to earth. He brought with him the noise of his viols. Viols are a type of lyre or harp with twelve strings and played on with the fingers (not with a plectrum). It comes from the Hebrew word 'nebel'. It is significant to note here that Isaiah's words do not state that God removed the musical instruments He had created within Satan when He expelled him from heaven. In fact, it can only be deduced that Satan fell to earth with his musical abilities within him.

Based on these musical abilities, the question to be posed is whether Satan still has the power to use music to influence the listener and whether Christian worshippers should be listening to non-Christian music.

It can be argued that not all music a Christian listens to should be listened to, nor is it beneficial. As we will read later, human beings are triune, and music affects all three parts of our being. Hence, we must be vigilant in what we allow ourselves to hear. Furthermore, it is not so much about the music that one consumes but rather if the music that person listens to begins to consume him or her for the better or worse.

There are many genres of music which have lyrics that contain subliminal messages leading the listener to do negative things such as serve Satan, take part in hedonistic activities, or even cause thoughts that lead to suicidal thoughts.

Subliminal messages can be of an even more sinister nature and cause real intentional harm to its listeners. For example in 1990, there was a legal case involving rock band Judas Priest, where two people took their lives in a suicide pact. Their parents attributed their death to a subliminal message 'do it' allegedly hidden in the Judas Priest song, 'Better By You, Better Than Me'. However, in this case the band was found not guilty.

Listening to non-Christian music may seem harmless to the Christian listener. After all, they ought to be able to filter out its harmful effects before they hit the mind. However, this theory is likened to the story of the boiling frog. In the world of biology, we are told if a frog is placed into boiling water, it will immediately jump out. Yet, if that same frog is put into a bowl of cool water and then slowly heated, the frog will eventually boil to death.

In the same vein, if a song is openly negative with dark hidden messages, it would be unlikely that any Christian would listen to it. However, as has been documented, many current popular music of varying genres actually contain hidden subliminal messages. These messages slowly embed themselves into the mind and soul of the listener, and the message of the song is firmly planted into that person's mind subconsciously.

Imagine this scenario. Your friend invites you over for a cup of tea and a chat. You get there and have your first cup of tea, which is made just as you like it and tastes great. A little while later, he offers you a second cup. You accept, follow him into his kitchen, and continue your conversation while he makes your tea. However, what you see next leaves you speechless. While your friend prepares your tea, he sneezes on the tea towel he uses to dry your cup. He then proceeds to lick the teaspoon before using it to put the sugar in your cup. Before adding the milk, he smells it to check if it is off and pulls a face of disgust, which most likely indicates that the milk is off. Your friend then takes a sip of the milk concentrating on tasting it. He then says to himself, "That'll do," and pours milk into your cup. Oblivious to what he is doing, your friend then says, "If you grab the biscuits, I'll bring your tea through!" Do you drink the second cup of tea?

This may seem like a stomach-churning scenario, but if we now relate this to music, the question I want you to seriously consider is whether you really know how the music you love to listen to is prepared? We do not know what goes on behind the scenes of many of the songs and music that we listen to. I am not just talking about how songs are physically created, recorded, and finally produced; I am talking about the spiritual influences that can in turn influence the listener. It is for this reason I would urge all listeners, especially

Christian listeners, to think seriously about this. Just because a song sounds good doesn't means that it is good for you. I believe that Christians should have a good grasp and understanding of what is meant by spiritual warfare. Remember that Paul teaches that there is a spiritual battle going on. 'For we do not wrestle against flesh and blood, but against principalities, against powers, against the rulers of the darkness of this age, against spiritual hosts of wickedness in the heavenly places' (Ephesians 6: 12). So in light of this, when listening to your favourite song, I encourage you to listen with an ear of discernment.

Therefore, to overcome this negative influence, James says we should submit to God, 'resist the devil, and he will flee from you. Draw nigh to God, and he will draw nigh to you' (James 4: 7–8). The Greek word for 'resist' is 'anthistēmi' which means to set one's self against, to withstand, resist, oppose. Hence, James was vehemently encouraging us to firmly oppose the strategies of Satan, who, as earlier stated, comes as an angel of light. Paul sums it up nicely by saying that the things we need to think on should be those which are positive and a good report (Philippians 4: 8). So it can be argued that the music choices made should be guided and directed by the Holy Spirit Himself.

When the pursuit of holiness becomes a daily practice, it is expected that the Christian will no longer be faced with tough decisions of whether to listen to this artist or that artist. The choice will be simple. Music that adversely affects that person will be eliminated from the playlist, and the music that helps and heals will be their primary choice.

If a person listens to a particular song (Christian or non-Christian) over and over again, eventually, that song will begin to affect the triune person. As such, it takes maturity and obedience to God's spirit to know what to listen to.

It is my opinion that the debate will always continue as to whether it is godly to combine Christian lyrics with contemporary music styles. Yet, I firmly believe if the lyrics are taken from God's word and glorify Him, we are fulfilling Jesus' command and leading others to praise God.

Because music is such a powerful tool, its primary use is to affect the emotions of the listener in order to communicate a particular message. This tool can be used to portray a positive message, for example, as found in Christian music or a song written to raise money for charity. Likewise, it can be used to present a negative message, such as songs written promoting misogynistic values.

The wise King Solomon used his talents of song writing and poetry. He excelled in his God-given wisdom above the other song writers and lyricists. The Bible states that he wrote 3,000 parables and poems, as well as writing 1,005 songs. The topics of his parables, poems, and songs included animals, birds, creeping things, and fish. The Bible states that people and kings came from all over the earth to hear composed works (1 Kings 4: 29–34). No doubt his aim and motivation was to praise God through his lyrics. What a way to worship and give praise to God!

Chapter 2

Musical Instruments in the Tanakh

In dissecting biblical text, it is said that Satan was the first created being to have music placed within him. The first human documented in the Bible to handle a musical instrument was Jubal. However, although Jubal may have been the human source of all musical instruments as we know them now, it can be argued that few Christians understand the true spiritual significance of the instruments used in worship.

If a true understanding is known of the spiritual significance of musical instruments, would this change the manner in which we worship? To answer the question, one must first investigate the different instruments and their meanings and symbolisms.

As stated earlier, music played a vital part in Hebrew culture within all aspects of life, from work to worship to military activities. Listed below are some of the most popular musical instruments in the Tanakh, which is better known as the Old Testament.

String Instruments

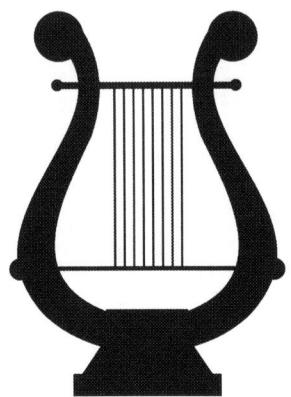

Harp/Lyre

The national instrument of the Hebrews had ten or eight strings, and it is first mentioned in Genesis 4: 21. Its Hebrew name is kinnor, and it symbolises praise and teaching some truths (Psalm 43: 3–4, Psalm 71: 22–23). It was used as an accompaniment to songs of cheerfulness as well as of praise to God (Genesis 31: 27; 1 Samuel 16: 23; 2 Chronicles 20: 28; Psalm 33: 2; and Psalm 137: 2). In 1 Chronicles 15: 21, mention is made of harps on the Sheminith to excel. The word 'Sheminith' means eighth or eight; this verse could mean they were harps that had eight strings.

Psaltery/Viol

This musical instrument is supposed to have been a kind of lyre or harp with twelve strings. Note here that the number twelve symbolises God's power, authority, and perfection of government or rule. The psaltery's Hebrew name is nebel, and it is first mentioned in 1 Samuel 10: 5 where it describes a group of prophets coming down from the hill of God. It is also translated as viol (Isaiah 5: 12 and Isaiah 14: 11).

Percussion Instruments

The Timbrel/Tabret
(Illustration by Pamela Fletcher)

It is an instrument played with the hand. It resembled and sounded like a minihand drum. Its Hebrew name is toph and is first mentioned in Genesis 31: 27. It symbolised a sign of victory and jubilee, usually played after a victory has been won. Interestingly, this is the name of one of the instruments that was created in Heylel (Ezekiel 28: 13).

The Bells

There are two Hebrew words in Scripture rendered "bell". The first Hebrew word is 'pa'amon', and the second is 'mĕtsillah'. Let me first talk about the pa'amon. These were small bells attached to the hem of the high priest's ephod. The purpose of the bells attached to the hem of high priest's robe was that as Aaron (the high priest) went to minister, he would be heard going in and out of the holy place and that he did not die. The bells were made of gold and attached to the hem next to small blue, purple, and scarlet pomegranates (Exodus 28: 33–35).

Gold symbolises the divinity of God, His righteousness, and the glory of Christ (Revelation 1: 12–13). The pomegranate fruit symbolises law and righteousness because it is said to have 613 seeds, which is equal to the 613 commandments of the Torah.

As such, when it is put together, when the bells on the High Priest's garments are heard, it reminds the people of God's divinity, His righteousness, and His law. Note that through Christ's death, we are the royal priesthood; however, the priestly garments we are encouraged to wear are not physical but spiritual. Firstly, we must put on Christ Himself (Romans 13: 14). Remember that through Christ's death, the law was abolished. He represents divinity, righteousness, and grace. When we put on Christ, we put on divinity, righteousness, and grace (Ephesians 2: 8). Secondly, we are to put on the whole armour of God (Ephesians 6: 11–17), of which each part represents Christ. Truth (John 14: 6), righteousness (1 Corinthians 1: 30), peace (Ephesians 2: 13–14), faith (Hebrews 12: 2), salvation (Luke 2: 25–30), and the Word of God (John 1: 1, 14 and Revelation 19: 13).

The second bell mentioned is in Zechariah 14:20, and its Hebrew name is mĕtsillah. It is a bell that is attached to the horse's bridle inscribed with 'Holiness unto the Lord.'

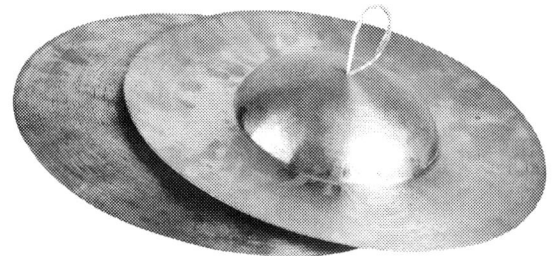

Cymbals

They were made of copper and the only percussion instrument in the temple orchestra. There were two types mentioned. The first is known by its Hebrew name 'mĕtseleth' and is first mentioned in 1 Chronicles 13: 8. They were used when the people were celebrating and praising God. They joined with trumpets and singers to express joy and thanks to the Lord (1 Chronicles 15: 16 and 16: 5). Asaph, David's chief musician (1 Chronicles 16: 5), was a cymbal player. When the builder's laid the foundation of the temple, one of the first instruments to be played by Asaph's descendants was the cymbals (Ezra 3: 10).

The second type of cymbals mentioned is the Hebrew word 'tsĕlatsal', first mentioned in 2 Samuel 6: 5. However, it is also found twice in Psalm 150: 5. Do not be confused. The first mention refers to the loud cymbals, which were small handheld cymbals equivalent to the castanets. The second mention is the high-sounding cymbals, which were larger handheld cymbals.

Cornet

There are two types of cornet. The first resembles a kind of rattle and is used as a musical instrument. Its Hebrew name is mĕna'na. It is not to be confused with the cornet of today. The mĕna'na is only mentioned once in the Bible, in 2 Samuel 6: 5. The second mention of the cornet is the Hebrew word 'showphar', which is the ram's horn (1 Chronicles 15: 28, Psalm 98: 6, and Hosea 5: 8).

Instrument of Music

An instrument of music refers to the Hebrew word 'shaliysh', the root of which means three or triple. Hence, it could be an instrument that maybe triangularly shaped. It is found only once in the Bible, in 1 Samuel 18: 6.

Wind Instruments

Pipes

There are three types of pipes mentioned throughout the Bible. The first is the organ. Its Hebrew name is ugab, and it is first mentioned in Genesis 4: 21. It is not to be confused with the organ of today, but in fact, it is a reed instrument with multiple pipes more akin to the panpipe or a bagpipe (Job 21: 12, Job 30: 31, and Psalm 150: 4). It derives from the Hebrew word 'agab', meaning to breathe and blow.

Next, the Hebrew word 'chaliyl' is translated as pipe due to it being perforated with holes. It derives from the Hebrew word 'chalal', meaning to bore through, to pierce, and to play the flute or pipe. It is first mentioned in 1 Samuel 10: 5, listed with instruments that the company of prophets played when they came down the hill prophesying. The chaliyl could produce bright sounds for joyous occasions (1 Kings 1: 40) as well as sad notes of grief (Jeremiah 48: 36).

The last mention of pipes is the Hebrew word 'neqeb', its English translation actually being pipes.

Interestingly, the neqeb appears only once throughout scripture, in Ezekiel 28: 13, in reference to an instrument created in Heylel by Yahweh. As such, unlike the ugab and chaliyl, which were made by human hands, the neqeb is a special instrument made solely by Yahweh's own hands. It was made with heavenly materials that have never been seen or even imagined by any human being. I believe it can be fairly assumed that the neqeb has never been played by any human being. What a holy item indeed!

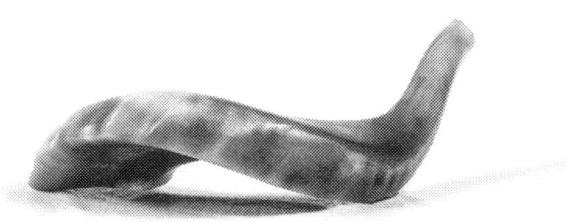

Trumpet

There are three words in Hebrew that can be translated as trumpet that were used by the Levitical priests.

1. Yowbel. The word 'trumpet' appears is in Exodus 19: 13. The Hebrew name is 'yowbel', which is interpreted as a ram's horn and was used on special occasions. The horn is an emblem of anointing, power, strength, dominion, glory, and fierceness. The yowbel is a picture of our salvation, and the horn of salvation applies to Christ who is our strong Saviour (Luke 1: 69). It denotes prosperity and triumph (Psalm 89: 17).

2. Showphar. The first time this word appears is in Exodus 19: 16. This word is both the same in English and Hebrew. It is literally a ram's horn and is rendered in the King James Version of the Bible as trumpet (sixty-eight times) and cornet (four times). Its root word is 'shaphar', which means 'to be pleasing, beautiful, bright, or glisten' and is mentioned only once, in Psalm 16: 6. It was used in spiritual warfare (Zechariah 9: 14 –15).

3. Chatsotserah. This word is rendered solely as trumpet twenty-nine times in the King James Version of the Bible. The initial two functions of the trumpets were the calling of assembly (the tekiah) and the breaking of camp (the teruah). The tekiah is a short blast of a single silver trumpet used to call the community to assemble with Moses at the entrance to the dwelling. The teruah is a series of rapid staccato blasts to signal the families that surrounded the tabernacle compound to move out (Numbers 10: 5, 6). They were made of silver, which symbolises righteousness and true words (Psalm 12: 6, Proverbs 10: 20 and 25: 11) and developing strength and faith (Psalm 66: 10) as well as redemption.

Clapping

Although not an actual physical instrument, clapping of the hands was used within worship. When we clap to applaud an achievement, it is the same as in the spiritual; the Holy Spirit leads God's people to clap as an outward show that God has done something specific on our behalf.

Psalm 47: 1 implores the worshipper to 'Oh, clap your hands, all you peoples! Shout to God with the voice of triumph!' but why? The psalmist explains that we are to clap because God is a great King over all the earth and that He shall subdue the nations under our feet and choose our inheritance for us (Psalm 47: 3–4). So in essence, we are saying to God, 'Bravo! He has done it.'

Voice and Singing

It is innate within mankind to sing, whether in the shower, whilst washing up, listening to the radio in the car, or even subconsciously singing a song that was heard in passing. So it should be of no surprise to find that throughout scripture, mankind communicated its praise to God through the voice and singing.

In fact, whenever God's people come together in corporate worship, it can be fairly assumed that a vast majority of the time, they will sing. Have you ever wondered why? It is not only that we just enjoy singing or even that we have a great voice to sing with. As many would profess, they do not. The question that one must ask is not does one have a great voice but rather does one have a song with which to worship the Lord?

Of course, I am not saying that God is not interested in the quality of the voice, but I am saying that in my opinion, He is interested in what we are saying to Him from the heart. In Psalm 47: 6, the author encourages the reader to 'Sing praises to God, sing praises! Sing praises to our King, sing praises!'. The instruction is not sing praises with excellent voice but simply to sing. In fact, throughout scripture, whenever God talks about the voice, He does not talk about its excellence in song. Rather, He talks about a voice of thanksgiving (Psalm 26: 7), a voice of joy and praise (Psalm 42: 4 and 118: 15), and a voice of triumph (Psalm 47: 1). The Bible does not record that God was or is interested in the quality of the voice.

Furthermore, the content of our songs are vitally important too. The Bible says in Psalm 138 that God magnifies His Word over His name. In addition to that, Jesus reminds us after heaven and earth fade away, it is His words that remain (Luke 21: 33). The scripture talks of how healing is found in the Word of God (Psalm 107: 20). It is God's word that brings light (Psalm 119: 105), and to live, we need the Word of God (Matthew 4: 4). Hence, when we sing, it is important to use or focus on the Word of God. Paul tells the Colossians:

> Let the word of Christ dwell in you richly in all wisdom, teaching and admonishing one another in psalms and hymns and spiritual songs, singing with grace in your hearts to the Lord. (Colossians 3: 16)

There is biblical evidence that records that Jesus Himself sang whilst on earth (Mark 14: 26). At the time He sang, Jesus knew that He was going to go through a testing time to say the least. This is a fantastic example for us to follow. When we are facing our personal tests, we are to sing!

However, what song did Jesus sing? We know from research and tradition that the Jews commemorated the Passover. This was an event whereby the angel of death sent to destroy the Egyptians passed over the house of the Jews because they had daubed their lintels and doorframes with the blood of a sacrificed lamb. Before the angel of death comes, they are told to prepare and eat a special meal in preparation for their miraculous deliverance (Exodus 12).

It can only be reasoned that in following and keeping the practises of the time, the song that Jesus sang was the Great Hallel, taken from Psalms 113 to 118 and Psalm 136. Further still, after completing my own research, I would deduce that at this time, the Song of Moses (Exodus 15) was also sung because it was written by Moses to specifically celebrate the deliverance of Israel. It was the first song to be sung after the first Passover meal. This first Passover meal was in fact foreshadowing the sacrifice of Jesus, the true Passover Lamb (1 Corinthians 5: 7, John 1: 35–36, and Acts 8: 32), whose blood protects those who accept him (Hebrews 9: 12–14).

Hence, it is even more poignant that Jesus did sing these songs confirmed by John the Divine, who gave an account of a vision whereby a time is coming when all shall worship and sing the song that Jesus sang; the song of the Lamb.

> And I saw something like a sea of glass mingled with fire, and those who have the victory over the beast, over his image and over his mark and over the number of his name, standing on the sea of glass, having harps of God. They sing the song of Moses, the servant of God, and the song of the Lamb, saying: "Great and marvelous are Your works, Lord God Almighty! Just and true are Your ways, O King of the saints! (Revelation 15: 2–3).

So what of the origins of music? The Bible affirms that everything in heaven and on earth was created by God (Colossians 1: 16, John 1: 3, and Ephesians 3: 9). One can deduce that this everything must include music. Furthermore, the Bible documents God's love for music, stating that He sings over his people (Zephaniah 3: 17) and in heaven music and singing surround Him day and night (Revelation 5: 9–14).

God's creation produces a musical composition for Him, and perhaps, it could be reasonably assumed that even the smallest particles are vibrating and resounding in music that God can hear and enjoy.

Based on the above, I would strongly suggest that the beginning of music from a biblical perspective was created by God Himself.

Chapter 3

Hebrew Words for Praise and Worship

It is important to note here that the Old Testament was originally written in Hebrew and the New Testament in Greek. In order to grasp the true meaning of any verse or chapter, it is important to study the rudimentary origins of the Hebrew or Greek word(s) of the passage of scripture that you are studying. Paul schools Timothy in 2 Timothy 2: 15 to "Be diligent to present yourself approved to God, a worker who does not need to be ashamed, rightly dividing the word of truth."

I personally make it a habit to separate my devotional time from my study time, which is why Paul encouraged Timothy to be diligent when studying the Word of God. Of course, my devotion and study time intertwine sometimes, but usually, my devotional time consists of reading God's word and praying to draw closer to God. It is all about relationship. My study time is my time to be enlightened and to grow in knowledge. Both devotional time and study time are a necessity for Christians in their daily walk with God (Philippians 3: 10 and Acts 17: 10–11). A contextual study establishes connotation.

In my opinion, the true meaning of praise and worship can be easily missed and misconstrued. In the Bible, these words have a few translations. Without looking at the original Hebrew or Greek words, you could possibly miss its precise meaning. Hence, it is important to understand the original meaning of the words and read them in context. Let me begin by giving my definition of the word 'praise'.

What is Praise?

To praise God is to give Him the respect He deserves by acknowledging and appreciating the great work He has done and to boast about His glory and magnificence.

Psalm 96: 3–5 says:

Declare His glory among the nations, His wonders among all peoples. For the LORD is great and greatly to be praised; He is to be feared above all gods. For all the gods of the peoples are idols, But the LORD made the heavens.

Throughout scripture, the praise of God is of high importance. When the Israelites praised Him, they were differentiating Him from all other gods that were worshipped at the time, defining Him as the only one worthy to be praised (Deuteronomy 4: 35; 2 Samuel 7: 22; and Isaiah 44: 8).

Hence, it is fair to say that praise in itself should be a function of the will and not only the emotions. The Bible stated that Jesus, whilst in the Garden of Gethsemane and going through anguish, even to the point that His sweat became drops of blood, still prayed to His Father and said, 'Father, if it is Your will, take this cup away from Me; nevertheless not My will, but Yours, be done' (Luke 22: 42). Jesus knew of the great plan of redemption that was predestined before the foundation of the earth, and He was willing to put aside His feelings to do the will of His Father. The Psalmist also expresses it clearly by declaring, 'Why are you cast down, O my soul? And why are you disquieted within me? Hope in God, for I shall yet praise Him For the help of His countenance.' (Psalm 42: 5). The Psalmist here felt cast down emotionally but still found it in him to praise God.

The question must then be asked of how one ought to praise God. There are many actions, supported biblically, that are involved with praise to God; we will look at these later on.

When we praise God, we show that we are being obedient to the word of God; it pleases Him, and above all, the Bible states that God inhabits the praise of Israel (Psalm 22: 3). Through Abraham, we are entitled to the same promise (Galatians 3: 29 and Ephesians 3: 6), so as we praise God, He inhabits our praise. The praise uttered by the worshipper should be in proportion to God's greatness, which means it has to be measureless. The more God is praised, the more His greatness is acknowledged.

Hebrew Words for Praise

- **Yadah.** This literally meaning to use (i.e., hold out) the hand or to physically throw out the hands and praise with extended hands. Our hands are an extension of our inward nature and an expression of a deep surrender to God, and it is an extension of our hearts desiring to exalt Him. Yadah praise is the giving of one's body, soul, and spirit in adoration. Do not be surprised when you see someone lifting his or her hands up in a time of praise. This is total submission to God, just as when a young child throws his hands out to his parent.

  Yadah is translated in the Old Testament into the following words: praise, give thanks, confess, thank, make confession,

27

thanksgiving, cast, cast out, shoot, and thankful. Here are some scriptures relating to a yadah praise: Genesis 29: 35; 2 Chronicles 7: 6; 20: 21; Psalm 9: 1, 28: 7, 33: 2, 42: 5 and 11, 49: 18, and 100: 4; and Isaiah 12: 1.

- **Towdah.** To praise with thanksgiving and to give worship by the extension of the hand in adoration or agreeing with what has been done or will be done. Towdah is translated in the Old Testament into the following words: thanksgiving, praise, thanks, thank offerings, and confession. Here are some scriptures relating to a towdah praise: Psalm 42: 4 and 50: 23 and Jeremiah 17: 26.

- **Halal.** This is the root for hallelujah and means to shine, boast over God, and celebrate foolishly. This type of praise is an abandonment of self. It speaks of the glorious attributes, workings, mercy, goodness, power, and love to God. Halal is translated in the Old Testament into the following words: praise, glory, boast, mad, shine, foolish, fools, commended, rage, celebrate, give, marriage, and renowned. Here are some scriptures relating to a halal praise: 2 Chronicles 20: 19; Psalm 22: 22–23; Isaiah 45: 25; Joel 2: 26; and Nahum 2: 4.

- **Tehillah.** This word means to sing a song of spontaneous praise, glorifying God in song. There are more than 300 times the worshipper is exhorted to sing with various Hebrew words meaning to sing. However, it is only the songs that flow from our spirits that are called tehillah praise. It implies to total involvement of oneself in praise to God (Psalm 65: 1 and 100: 4). Isaiah confirms that it is music that is the healer to the soul stating that the Spirit of God has given a garment of tehillah to replace the "spirit of heaviness" (Isaiah 61: 3).

Tehillah has only one translation in the Old Testament. This is praise, and we know that these are songs or hymns of praise! Here are some scriptures relating to a tehillah praise: Nehemiah 12: 46; Psalm 33: 1 and 145: 21; Jeremiah 49: 25; and Zephaniah 3 :20.

- **Shabach.** This means to address in a loud voice or tone or to shout, command, triumph, or glory with a loud voice. The phrase "shout unto the Lord" can be understood as the action of Shabach. Have you ever praised God to a stage that you have shouted out, "Thank you, Jesus!"? You have just entered the Shabach zone of praise! Shabach is translated in the Old Testament into the following words: praise, still, keep it in, glory, triumph, and commend. Here are some scriptures relating to a shabach praise: 1 Chronicles 16: 35; Psalm 63: 3, 117: 1, and 147: 12; and Proverbs 29: 11.

- **Barak.** This word means to kneel or bow down and to bless God or to give reverence to God as an act of adoration. It implies a continual, conscious acknowledgment of God – an attitude of expectancy, in a worshipful attitude expecting to receive (Psalm 72: 15). It is often rendered as the words 'bless' or 'blessed' (Psalm 145: 1; Proverbs 22: 9; and Jeremiah 17: 7). Barak is often translated in the Old Testament into the following words: bless, salute, curse, blaspheme, blessing, praised, kneel down, congratulate, kneel, and make to kneel. Here are some scriptures relating to a barak praise: Genesis 1: 28 and 1 Chronicles 18: 10.

- **Zamar.** This means to touch the strings or to sing and play with instruments. Translated many times as 'sing praises', this kind of praise is mostly rejoicing (2 Samuel 22: 50; Psalm 33:

2; and Isaiah 12: 5). Zamar is translated in the Old Testament into the following words: praise, sing, sing psalms, and sing forth. Here are some other scriptures relating to a zamar praise: Judges 5: 3 and Psalm 9:11 and 144: 9.

Below you can see how in Hebrew we have a more specific explanation of the expressions of praise.

"The Levites, from the sons of the Kohathites and of the sons of the Korahites, stood up to praise **[halal]** the LORD God of Israel, with a very loud voice. When he had consulted with the people, he appointed those who sang to the LORD and those who praised **[halal]** Him in holy attire, as they went out before the army and said, "Give thanks **[yadah]** to the LORD, for His lovingkindness is everlasting." When they began singing and praising **[tehillah]**, the LORD set ambushes against the sons of Ammon, Moab and Mount Seir, who had come against Judah; so they were routed." (2 Chronicles 20: 19, 21–22 [NASB])

What is Worship?

To worship God is the response we reflect back to Him for what He has revealed to us about Himself through His Son Jesus Christ (Hebrews 1: 2–3), through His Holy Spirit (1 Corinthians 2: 10), through scripture (John 1: 1), and through nature (Romans 1: 20). This revelation is His glory.

Worship is likened unto this; just as the moon reflects the sunlight, so the Church reflects the character of God through its worship of Him. However, note mankind can only reflect God's righteousness (Philippians 3: 9) because mankind can only be covered by Christ's righteousness (1 Corinthians 1: 30). We cannot generate righteousness of our own self (Isaiah 64: 6); it is a gift from God (Romans 5:17).

There are many ways in which we are called to express our worship to God, and these can be better seen by analysing the original Hebrew for the word 'worship' found in the Old Testament.

Hebrew Words for Worship

- **Shachah.** This word means to depress or prostrate oneself in homage to God by bowing, falling down flat, and throwing oneself down before someone. It is translated in the Old Testament as worship, bow, bow down, obeisance, reverence, fall down, stoop, and crouch. Here are some other scriptures relating to a shachah worship: Genesis 18: 2; Exodus 12: 27; Judges 7: 15; and 1 Chronicles 16: 29.

  Cĕgid. This word also means to prostrate oneself in homage, fall down, or worship. Although it seems to have the same meaning as shachah, this type of worship refers only to the worshipping of idols and not the true and living God. Can you see how again this highlights the important of recognising the original meaning of a word? Cĕgid has only one translation in the Old Testament. This is worship and appears only in the book of Daniel with reference to worshipping the golden image that Nebuchadnezzar had built: Daniel 3: 5–7, 10–12, 14–15, 18, and 28.

Chapter 4

Greek Words for Praise and Worship

In the previous chapter, definitions for the words 'praise' and 'worship' were given. To help get a better understanding of the type of praise and worship used in the New Testament, I will now analyse the original Greek words used.

Greek Words for Praise

- **Ainesis.** This word refers to praising with a thanks offering. Ainesis has only one translation in the New Testament, and this is praise. The only time it is referred to in scripture is in Hebrews 13: 15, where the writer encourages the reader to offer a sacrifice of praise to God.

- **Aineo.** This word means to praise, extol, and to sing praises in honour to God. Aineo has only one translation in the New Testament, and this is praise. Some scriptures featuring an aineo type of praise are Luke 2: 13; Acts 2: 47; Romans 15: 11; and Revelation 19: 5.

- **Ainos.** This means a laudatory praise of God, expressing praise in commendation. Ainos has only one translation in the New Testament, and this is praise. This type of praise can only be found twice in scripture: Matthew 21: 16 and Luke 18: 43.

- **Epaineo.** This word means to laud or praise God highly in a public setting. It is translated in the New Testament as praise, laud, and commend and can be found in the following scriptures Luke 16: 8; Romans 15: 11; and 1 Corinthians 11: 2, 17, and 22.

- **Epainos.** This word means to give laudation, commendation, and praise. Epainos has only one translation in the New Testament, and this is praise. It can be found in numerous verses such as Romans 2: 29; 1 Corinthians 4: 5; Philippians 1: 11 and 4: 8; and 1 Peter 2: 14.

- **Hymneo.** This word means to sing the praises of and sing hymns to God. It is translated as to sing a hymn and sing praise. Furthermore, it also relates to the Jewish tradition of the singing of the paschal hymns (hymns celebrating the Passover). These hymns are found in Psalms 113 to 118 and Psalm 136 and known as the great Hallel. In the New Testament, hymneō praise is mentioned four times: Matthew 26: 30, Mark 14: 26; Acts 16: 25; and Hebrews 2: 12.

I want us to focus on the word 'worship' and how it is translated in the New Testament.

Greek Words for Worship

- **Proskyneo.** This word originally carried with it the idea of someone falling down to kiss the ground before a king or a king's feet. Its literal definition is to kiss, like a dog licking his master's hand, to fawn or crouch to, and to give homage (do reverence to, adore). Proskyneō has only one translation in the New Testament, and this is worship. Some examples are Matthew 2: 2; John 4: 23–24; Hebrews 1: 6; and Revelation 11: 16 and 13: 4.

- **Sebo.** This word means to revere or to hold in awe. It is often translated as worship, devout, and religious. Some examples of sebō worship can be found in the following verses: Matthew 15: 9; Mark 7: 7; and Acts 16: 14 and 18: 7.

- **Latreuo.** This word means to minister to God, render religious service of homage, serve, and do the service of worship. It is often translated as serve, worship, do the service, and worshipper. It actually derives from the Greek word 'latris', meaning a hired menial worker. Therefore, it is why it means to serve. Note that we are God's servants, or His doulos, and as such, this type of worship should be a part of our being! Examples of a latreuo type of worship can be found in Matthew 4: 10; Philippians 3: 3; 2 Timothy 1: 3; and Revelation 7: 15.

- **Eusebo.** This word means to act piously or reverently towards God. It is translated as worship and show piety and is found twice in scripture: Acts 17: 23 and 1 Timothy 5: 4.

- **Ethelothreskeia.** This is voluntarily or arbitrary worship. Unlike free will worship of God, this type of worship is said to be misdirected zeal. It is also translated as will worship in the New Testament and is found in only one scripture: Colossians 2: 23. Here, Paul questions the brethren as to why they follow rules and regulations that are purely pious and religious but do not help a person to overcome their personal problems.

Jesus clearly instructs us as to how we are to worship God from the triune man perspective. It should be done in spirit and in truth – i.e., not in the flesh (body) or from emotions (soul) but from the inner man (spirit). However, we should still present our bodies as a living sacrifice, holy and acceptable to God.

Furthermore, Jesus encourages us to worship in truth, which is the Greek word alētheia. This is a truth as is taught concerning respecting God and the execution of His purposes through Christ. It is this truth that respects the duties of man and opposes the superstitions of the Gentiles, the inventions of the Jews, and the corrupt opinions and precepts of false teachers, even among Christians. Our worship is to be done through Jesus, who is the Truth (John 14: 6), and in accordance with God's word, which is the truth (John 17: 17). The importance of the word of God cannot be underestimated as it is imperative to note that our worship is no higher than our knowledge of God as worship flows from our relationship with Him. Our relationship with Him is only strengthened by learning of Him through His word.

God knows our heart and intentions, and He knows when worship is false. Matthew records Jesus' words as such:

> These people draw near to Me with their mouth, And honor Me with their lips,
> But their heart is far from Me. And in vain they worship Me, Teaching as doctrines the commandments of men. (Matthew 15: 8–9).

Jesus highlights the fact that there were people who were worshipping God for other people to hear ("with their lips") and with no focus on God ("their heart is far from me"). This type of worship He describes is vain or fruitless, as meant by the original Greek word 'matēn'.

The worship God requires is a result of an intimate, giving, and receiving relationship with God. As the worshipper opens his or her heart to God, he receives the permission to move forward into God's presence to have fellowship with Him.

Overall, praise means to commend, to applaud, or to magnify, and praise to God is an expression of worship, lifting up, and glorifying God. It is argued that in accordance with scripture, human beings were created to praise and worship the Creator: "This people I have formed for Myself; They shall declare My praise." (Isaiah 43: 21).

> But you are a chosen generation, a royal priesthood,
> a holy nation, His own special people, that you may
> proclaim the praises of Him who called you out of
> darkness into His marvelous light (1 Peter 2: 9).

I believe it is innate within mankind to praise God as that is how we were created; after all, the creator cannot worship its creation. In fact, the Bible tells us that worship takes place on a grand scale by the angels, who were also created by God (John 1: 3 and Colossians 1: 16). Here are some scriptures that reflect this: Isaiah 6: 1–3; Luke 2: 12–14; Revelation 4: 8–10; and Revelation 7: 11. Thus, if angels worship God, how much more should mankind who are made a little lower than the angels (Hebrews 2: 7)?

However, when the purpose of mankind is shirked, they seek to praise and worship other things, as Paul explains in Romans 1: 25: "Who exchanged the truth of God for the lie, and worshiped and served the creature rather than the Creator, who is blessed forever. Amen."

To conclude, I would like to encourage you to ask yourself the following question: Do I give more honour to the song rather than to the subject of the song that I sing?

Chapter 5

Prophetic Praise and Conflict Resolution

As in all walks of life, when a group of people come together to work on the same goal, conflicts do arise. Do not think because the worship team are Christians that there is exemption to the rule. If two of the greatest apostles, Peter and Paul, had a disagreement (Galatians 2: 11–21), then what more your worship band? Conflicts can create a barrier to the prophetic flowing in your praise and worship ministry. As such, in this chapter, I aim to help you gain a better understanding of prophetic praise and worship and how discernment is a vital element of this ministry. Finally, I will also discuss how conflict can be managed and resolved.

Prophetic Praise and Worship

It is said that spontaneous praise and worship is prophetic. This is true. However, in my opinion, I believe prophetic praise and worship is misunderstood. I will be going into that shortly, but I want to talk about spontaneous praise and worship. When we refer to spontaneous, it often means something that is done on the spot or is improvised, so with regards to spontaneous praise and worship, it is often understood as the worship leaders and musicians creating music, words, and the melody as they are inspired. This may sound like a new phenomenon in worship but actually it is biblical. In Psalm 149: 1, it states, "Praise the LORD! Sing to the LORD a new song, And His praise in the assembly of saints."

On a number of occasions, we are encouraged in scripture to sing a new song. When we look at the word 'new', this is the Hebrew word 'chadash', חָדָשׁ which means new, new thing, and fresh. The root word means to be new, renew, and repair. To sing a new song clearly means to create a new song or to bring a renewing to a song that is already known. God, by His Holy Spirit, can inspire us during praise and worship to write new songs and music and also to have new ideas, but the focus must be to bring glory to God. What we do must be biblically sound and must testify of the supremacy of Christ.

Every worshipper should be aware of the power of prophetic praise and worship within the spiritual realm. It is a weapon of warfare given by God to help us in our walk. The weapon I refer to, which is at the believer's disposal, is the word of God (Ephesians 6: 17).

As we have previously looked at the words for praise and worship, let us now look briefly at the word 'prophetic'. Most people would rightly say that a prophetic word is about revealing the future. This is correct, but it is much deeper than that. The word 'prophet' is the noun of prophetic, and in Hebrew, it's the word 'naba', which means to prophesy (sing or speak by inspiration), one who reveals or declares the words of God to man, and one who speaks by a divine authority. Having taken this into consideration, the Bible declares that we ought to ' …worship God! for the testimony of Jesus is the spirit of prophecy' (Revelation 19: 10). So to move prophetically in praise and worship is to reveal Jesus Christ.

To put it another way, as we witness about Christ and His saving power, we release the spirit of prophecy into people's lives and change their circumstance for the better. Yes, a Word from God can actually change our lives. In 1 Samuel chapter 10, it says:

> After that you shall come to the hill of God where the Philistine garrison is. And it will happen, when you have come there to the city, that you will meet a group of prophets coming down from the high place with a stringed instrument, a tambourine, a flute, and a harp before them; and they will be prophesying. Then the Spirit of the LORD will come upon you, and you will prophesy with them and be turned into another man.
> (1 Samuel 10: 5–6)

Notice the scripture here says that a group of prophets were prophesying with instruments, and as they prophesy, Saul will prophesy with them. As he prophesies, Saul is told he will be turned into a different man. Obviously, this must mean for the better.

What does the Bible mean when it says we prophesy with instruments? (Also, see 1 Chronicles 25: 1). Let me explain. Earlier, we read in Revelation 19: 10 that 'the testimony of Jesus is the spirit of prophecy.' In other words, we could say that witnessing about Jesus releases the spirit of prophecy. Whether through song, musical instruments, speaking, or indeed any other way that glorifies and brings attention to Christ, in essence, we are prophesying into the spiritual realm, which will bring revelation to those who are witnesses to our attestation of Christ.

When revelation comes, it will bring a change to your life. It will revolutionise and rejuvenate you. In other words, you will be a different person to the person you were before receiving the revelation. We need to remember that all prophecy comes from God, inspired by the Holy Ghost (2 Peter 1: 21). Jesus Himself tells us that the very words He speaks are spirit and life (John 6: 63).

We can see the importance of prophecy throughout the Bible, and one of my personal favourite prophecies is in Ezekiel 37: 1–14 when God speaks to Ezekiel in a vision and tells him to prophesy to the dry bones. The first stage was to prophesy to the bones for flesh and sinew to come upon them, and it did. The second time he prophesied is when God told him to prophesy that breath would come into the bodies, and it did. Finally, he prophesied that they would be brought up out of their graves and given life; this was a word of prophecy for the future.

Today, we can change people's lives when we make ourselves available to God. Remembering the prophecy by Joel (Joel 2: 28), which was preached on the day of Pentecost by Peter.

> And it shall come to pass in the last days, says God, That I will pour out of My Spirit on all flesh; Your sons and your daughters shall prophesy, Your young men shall see visions, Your old men shall dream dreams. And on My menservants and on My maidservants I will pour out My Spirit in those days; And they shall prophesy. (Acts 2: 16–18)

Every worshipper should be aware of the power of praise and worship within the spiritual realm. As already mentioned, it is a weapon of warfare given by God for His people to help them to overcome their enemy.

> For through the voice of the LORD Assyria will be beaten down, As He strikes with the rod. And in every place where the staff of punishment passes, Which the LORD lays on him, It will be with tambourines and harps; And in battles of brandishing He will fight with it. (Isaiah 30: 31–32).

Verse 32 reads with more clarity when one looks at it from the New Living Translation Version:

> And as the Lord strikes them with his rod of punishment, his people will celebrate with tambourines and harps. Lifting his mighty arm, he will fight the Assyrians.

This is clearly telling us that God Himself uses music to go forward and defeat the enemy of His people. When I refer to an enemy I'm talking of the spiritual realm. Paul states,

> For we do not wrestle against flesh and blood, but against principalities, against powers, against the rulers of the darkness of this age, against spiritual hosts of wickedness in the heavenly places. (Ephesians 6: 12)

Furthermore, the power of praise and worship can literally set a person free. Even though Paul and Silas were imprisoned and in chains, they still had a freedom. In fact, they began to sing songs of praise – to be more specific, it was songs of deliverance. We know this by the Greek word 'hymneo', which was used to describe singing praises. Hymneō were the hymns used to celebrate the Passover (Acts 16: 25–26).

However, as well as being a spiritual weapon, through praise and worship, we hear the prophetic voice of God. Lockyer Jr states in his book, 'All the Music of the Bible', 'music affects us, deeply, powerfully and prophetically.'

It is paramount for the worshipper, especially those that lead, to move prophetically in praise and worship. This occurs when we follow the leading of the Holy Spirit, and the reason is obvious, well at least it should be. The Bible declares,

> But as it is written: "Eye has not seen, nor ear heard, Nor have entered into the heart of man The things which God has prepared for those who love Him." But God has revealed them to us through His Spirit. For the Spirit searches all things, yes, the deep things of God. For what man knows the things of a man except the spirit of the man which is in him? Even so no one knows the things of God except the Spirit of God. (1 Corinthians 2: 9–11)

> Also, see Romans 8: 14.

Establishment and Discernment

The Bible teaches that the Holy Spirit knows exactly what God our Father has for us, the deep things of God. However, we must ask how we ought to tap in to the deep things of God. In order to know what is happening within the spiritual realm, the worshipper must be sensitive to the leading of the Holy Spirit. This involves selflessness, humility, and spending time alone in the presence of God (Matthew 6: 6). However, from my studies, I have deduced that there are two more essential factors that are necessary: establishment and discernment.

Let me first explain what it is to be established from a biblical point of view. In Hebrew, the word 'establish' is 'kuwn'. This means to be firm, stable, established, secure, and confirmed. From a biblical perspective, there are two ways in which we should be established. Primarily, we should be established by God (1 Kings 2: 45 and 1 Samuel 13: 13) and subsequently by Godly leaders (a pastor or deacon) (2 Chronicles 12: 1). Furthermore, we must refrain from disrespecting or disobeying Godly leadership; instead, we ought to pray for the leaders, asking God to grant them the wisdom to lead.

It goes without saying that if a Godly leader is directing or teaching you to do something that is contrary to the Bible, which is the word of God, and it is clearly not in line with the teachings of the Bible, our first duty is to obey God. This is clearly stated in the Bible where Peter and the other apostles were brought before the council of high priests.

> And when they had brought them, they set them before the council. And the high priest asked them, saying, "Did we not strictly command you not to teach in this name? And look, you have filled Jerusalem with your doctrine, and intend to bring this Man's blood on us!" But Peter and the other apostles answered and said: "We ought to obey God rather than men. (Acts 5: 27–29)

We must remember that whatever we listen to, whether in teaching or preaching of the word of God, or whatever literature we read or write, even when singing, our benchmark must be the undiluted word of God. We must avoid having itching ears and avoid listening to fables. Itching ears is a figure of speech used in scripture to describe a person who pursues dogmas that condone their lifestyle. A fable is a myth, which is generally believed but founded on a fictitious idea.

> Preach the word! Be ready in season and out of season. Convince, rebuke, exhort, with all longsuffering and teaching. For the time will come when they will not endure sound doctrine, but according to their own desires, because they have itching ears, they will heap up for themselves teachers; and they will turn their ears away from the truth, and be turned aside to fables (2 Timothy 4: 2–4)

After we have heard the teaching and preaching, it is imperative that we take time to study the scriptures. This was a norm for the people of Berea, and this must be our standard!

> These were more fair-minded than those in Thessalonica, in that they received the word with all readiness, and searched the Scriptures daily to find out whether these things were so. (Acts 17: 11)

Also, it is important to mention the role of leadership. It is easy to feel so enthusiastic about serving God in ministry that we jump ahead of ourselves and go into ministry where your pastor or your Godly leader has not officially given you the authority. Yes, it is true that personalities may clash from time to time and that misunderstandings and disagreements will happen, but leaders are there to watch over our souls (Hebrews 13: 17).

The Bible teaches us to wait on our call (Romans 12: 3–8). It is often said that patience is a virtue; indeed, patience is being prepared to wait for something without being irritated or anxious. As Paul admonishes us in Philippians 4: 6–7:

> Be anxious for nothing, but in everything by prayer and supplication, with thanksgiving, let your requests be made known to God; and the peace of God, which surpasses all understanding, will guard your hearts and minds through Christ Jesus.

Now let's look at the second essential factor: discernment.

Many of us miss the importance and the connection between the gift of discernment and worship. The two do go hand in hand, but you may ask how this is possible.

It is imperative for any worship leader leading a congregation to ask God for the gift of discernment in order to lead God's people into a fuller participation of true worship. Amongst other things, the gift of discernment will allow you to detect any unwanted spirit that is not of God, which has been sent to disrupt and cause confusion. Let us take note of what John says in 1 John 4: 1: "Beloved, do not believe every spirit, but test the spirits, whether they are of God; because many false prophets have gone out into the world."

The word 'test' here is the Greek word 'dokimazō', which means to test, examine, approve, prove, discern, or allow.

A great example of this in the Bible is one of the worship leaders installed by David. His name was Chenaniah, which actually means, 'Jehovah establishes.' Evidently, the Holy Spirit wants to reveal to us through scripture that Chenaniah was established or set up by God.

Of Chenaniah, it is said, ' ...was instructor in charge of the music, because he was skillful' (1 Chronicles 15: 22).

In this context, the Hebrew word for 'skillful' is 'biyn', and this means 'to discern, to understand, and to consider.' Hence, Chenaniah was a person who was able to discern and understand in order to lead the people in worship. This is of vital importance, and the gift of discernment is of no lesser importance in today's worship. I would argue that without this gift, our worship is in jeopardy of being attacked by the darkening forces of Satan as he seeks every way in which to disrupt our praise and worship towards God. Chenaniah would have known which songs to choose; he would have understood when to stop singing and when to continue singing. It can be argued that just because a person can sing beautifully does not mean they can sing skilfully. However, God does require us to sing skilfully, which is with discernment.

Moving in the prophetic in worship is not a new experience. Prophetic worship was evident throughout the Bible. For example, David installed Asaph as a worship leader. Asaph is the author of twelve Psalms and is an intriguing man with an even more intriguing ministry. In 1 Chronicles 16, it says:

> And he appointed some of the Levites to minister before the ark of the LORD, to commemorate, to thank, and to praise the LORD God of Israel: ⁵ Asaph the chief, and next to him Zechariah, then Jeiel, Shemiramoth, Jehiel, Mattithiah, Eliab, Benaiah, and Obed-Edom: Jeiel with stringed instruments and harps, but Asaph made music with cymbals; (1 Chronicles 16: 4–5)

This scripture clearly explains that Asaph was the head music minister among the Levites before the ark of God. 1 Chronicles 25 states:

> Moreover David and the captains of the army separated for the service some of the sons of Asaph, of Heman, and of Jeduthun, who should prophesy with harps, stringed instruments, and cymbals. And the number of the skilled men performing their service was: Of the sons of Asaph: Zaccur, Joseph, Nethaniah, and Asharelah; the sons of Asaph were under the direction of Asaph, who prophesied according to the order of the king. (1 Chronicles 25: 1–2).

Asaph and his sons prophesied to the accompaniment of lyres, harps, and cymbals, and he was involved in what we would describe today as prophetic worship. 2 Chronicles 29 confirms for us that Asaph was not just a worshipper but also a seer or prophet.

> Moreover King Hezekiah and the leaders commanded the Levites to sing praise to the LORD with the words of David and of Asaph the seer. So they sang praises with gladness, and they bowed their heads and worshiped. (2 Chronicles 29: 30)

Other examples of how God spoke prophetically to His servants who were sensitive to His voice include Moses replicating the heavenly tabernacle on the earth as God had shown and instructed him (Exodus Chapters 24 to 40), Gideon defeating the Midianites (Judges 7), the fall of the walls of Jericho (Joshua Chapters 5 and 6), and the victory of King Jehoshaphat and the Israelites (2 Chronicles

20). Also, the book of Psalms contains many prophetic prayers, praises, and declarations.

Joshua was given specific instructions by "the captain of the Lord's host" to take Jericho (Joshua 5: 14 and 6: 2). The children of Israel were to march around the city once for six days in silence with only the trumpet of the ram's horns sounding. Then, on the seventh day, they were to march around the city seven times. On the seventh time, with the long blast of the trumpets, they were to give a great shout. Joshua told the people, 'Shout, for the Lord has given you the city!' (Joshua 6: 16). As the sound of the trumpets and the great shout resounded in unison, the walls of Jericho fell (Joshua 6: 20).

The fall of the wall was a direct result of prophetic worship. The obedience and final cry of the people was a sign to their enemy that the plans and actions of heaven were at work. This was the partnership between God and His people at work. Often, as in the aforementioned example, prophetic worship does not make sense to the natural mind, but our trust must be in the Lord (Proverbs 3: 5–6).

The children of Israel responded to God's word in faith through obedience, and the direct result was the fall of the walls of Jericho, leading to them taking the land that had been promised to them.

Intimacy in worship is imperative within prophetic worship in order for the worshipper to draw closer to God. In the New Testament, one of the most commonly used words for worship is the word 'proskyneō.' It means to come towards to kiss. So in this type of worship, you have the picture of reverence, but within that reverence, there is closeness and a calling for you to approach God as if to offer Him a kiss. There is a sense in which the prophetic flows from that place of intimacy with God. You have to be close to God to hear His voice as He speaks with a whisper. We reflect on the story of how He spoke to Elijah in his time of deep depression.

> Then He said, "Go out, and stand on the mountain before the LORD." And behold, the LORD passed by, and a great and strong wind tore into the mountains and broke the rocks in pieces before the LORD, but the LORD was not in the wind; and after the wind an earthquake, but the LORD was not in the earthquake; and after the earthquake a fire, but the LORD was not in the fire; and after the fire a still small voice. (1 Kings 19: 11–12)

If a worshipper is to sing, play, or dance prophetically, this ministry has to come from having a relationship and being close to God, where the worshipper hears His voice and they become His spokesperson.

People are ushered into the Lord's presence through the prophecy in the music and in the words spoken. However, it is important to identify the fact that every prophet is subject to his own spirit (1 Corinthians 14: 32). That is to say that he or she is able to prophecy with understanding and wisdom. For this reason, we are not loose cannons unable to stop what is leaving our mouths. We are more likened to a running tap that one can turn on or off at will. As such, the prophetic worship ministry should operate in the same manner. The worshipper must know when and how to prophesy with understanding and wisdom. We must wait for our turn and be alert to the best moment to participate. Paul the Apostle, author of the letter to the Corinthians, said that he himself knew the importance of singing in the spirit and with understanding (1 Corinthians 14: 15) in order to avoid confusion (1 Corinthians 14: 33 and 40).

Moving in the prophetic worship ministry is for the purpose of edifying the church with the will and word of God. Hence, if one follows Paul's instructions in his letter to the Corinthians, it can be clearly seen that Paul was encouraging the church to use wisdom when worshipping in tongues (1 Corinthians 14). If a person does speak in tongues, he or she should wait for an interpretation (1 Corinthians 14:13). However, above this, Paul places more weight on the gift of prophecy as he sees this of greater value and edification to the church (1 Corinthians 14:5–6).

To conclude, the prophetic worship music ministry has a valid and imperative place within worship, as God loves worship and loves music. David wrote concerning God, 'You are my hiding place; You shall preserve me from trouble; You shall surround me with songs of deliverance.' (Psalm 32: 7). Hence, it is the glorifying of God that brings about the breakthrough and that lifts the oppressed believer. The Psalmist says, 'He sent His word and healed them, And delivered them from their destructions.' (Psalm 107: 20).

Thus, the reason why it is imperative that we use the word of God when we worship is because He has said that He has sent it to specifically help His people. Furthermore, He cannot go back on His word (Numbers 23: 19). God will always act upon His word (2 Peter 3: 9).

As previously stated, to move prophetically, one must spend intimate time in the presence of the Lord in order for the ministry of prophetic worship to be an outflow from one's life. It is of uttermost importance that worship leaders and musicians set aside and dedicate their personal time in the presence of the Lord.

A church could be populated with excellent musicians and singers who can sing and play to perfection, inspiring songs with excellent rifts and harmonies. However, without the anointing of the Holy Spirit, these tools are ineffective. God is not impressed with our talents or music. He desires our hearts.

Conflict Resolution

> 'Now I appeal to Euodia and Syntyche. Please, because
> you belong to the Lord, settle your disagreement.'
> (Philippians 4: 2; NLT)

Paul admonishes two women in Philippians 4: 2 to settle a disagreement that they had with each other. We are not told in the Bible what the disagreement was but the fact is Paul was all for conflict resolution. Let us take a look at what the Bible says about it.

What happens if a disagreement takes place within the praise and worship team, and what is the best way of resolving it? Before I delve into the question, it has to be said that the praise and worship team are an integral part of the church body. When conflict within the praise and worship team occurs, it could have an effect on the wider church. It is important to say that from a spiritual point of view, the worship team is at the forefront of the battle.

> And when he had consulted with the people, he
> appointed those who should sing to the Lord, and who
> should praise the beauty of holiness, as they went out
> before the army and were saying: "Praise the Lord,
> For His mercy endures forever." Now when they began
> to sing and to praise, the Lord set ambushes against

the people of Ammon, Moab, and Mount Seir, who had come against Judah; and they were defeated. (2 Chronicles 20: 21–22)

It is clear that when we look throughout scripture that praise and worship alters and influences the spiritual realm and creates an atmosphere in the natural that is conducive for worship and leads us ultimately into victory. The battle in which we are engaged is not against flesh and blood.

> For we do not wrestle against flesh and blood, but against principalities, against powers, against the rulers of the darkness of this age, against spiritual hosts of wickedness in the heavenly places. (Ephesians 6: 12)

With that in mind, let's go back to the original question: What happens if or when a disagreement takes place within the praise and worship team, and what is the best way of resolving it?

It is important to have a conversation about the situation soon after it transpires. This may be done initially on a one-to-one basis with the person with whom you are upset and without the interference of people who aren't involved. Depending on the circumstances, the leader could take the two aside, or the leader could talk to the group as a whole. Either way, talking about the situation as soon as possible is key (Matthew 5: 25). Doing this will eradicate gossip from escalating and getting out of hand. This must be done in love, preferring one another (Romans 12: 10).

If possible, attempt to bring a resolution before the day is out. 'Be angry, and do not sin": do not let the sun go down on your wrath' (Ephesians 4: 26).

Sometimes, we have to agree to disagree.

> Again I say, don't get involved in foolish, ignorant arguments that only start fights. A servant of the Lord must not quarrel but must be kind to everyone, be able to teach, and be patient with difficult people. (2 Timothy 2: 23–24; NLT)

We must endeavour to see the other person's viewpoint. Try to see where the other person is coming from. Recognise that everyone has been created differently with abilities, various gifts, and personality traits. Remember that each individual is unique and needs to be appreciated. 'Accept other believers who are weak in faith, and don't argue with them about what they think is right or wrong' (Romans 14: 1; NLT).

Initiate resolution. Be the first person in a disagreement to apologise for your part. Even when you think the other person is wrong, it's not a bad thing to apologise for offending the other person. Be genuine with your words in the process of resolving a dispute. 'Let no corrupt word proceed out of your mouth, but what is good for necessary edification, that it may impart grace to the hearers.' (Ephesians 4: 29).

Remember that the kingdom of God is more important than any disagreement. Serve God and do not forget that we have all sinned and fallen short of His glory. Be willing to see the bigger picture. Spending time working through conflict has a worthwhile reward and causes a deeper relationship in the end. Try not to blame or use accusing words: 'for all have sinned and fall short of the glory of God, being justified freely by His grace through the redemption that is in Christ Jesus' (Romans 3: 23–24).

Be thoughtful and understanding. Try to give answers when appropriate but know when to listen. Do not undervalue the importance of a listening ear. 'So then, my beloved brethren, let every man be swift to hear, slow to speak, slow to wrath;' (James 1: 19).

The most essential thing is to show love and forgiveness. Remember that no matter how bad things turn out during a dispute, revenge is not a path we must take. Pursue peace at all times where possible (Hebrews 12: 14).

> Since God chose you to be the holy people he loves, you must clothe yourselves with tenderhearted mercy, kindness, humility, gentleness, and patience. Make allowance for each other's faults, and forgive anyone who offends you. Remember, the Lord forgave you, so you must forgive others. Above all, clothe yourselves with love, which binds us all together in perfect harmony. (Colossians 3: 12–14; NLT)

Resolving conflict in any friendship is not the most pleasant task, but it is worth the hassle. The result on the other end is a deeper friendship. 'Wounds from a sincere friend are better than many kisses from an enemy' (Proverbs 27: 6; NLT).

However, if there is absolutely no way of compromise and the disputes gets out of hand, a time away from the worship team or expulsion is needed. However, this should occur only if all other avenues have been exhausted (Matthew 18: 15–20).

Chapter 6

The Role of the Levites in the Old Testament

We have already discussed that music was created by God and that music is very important to Him. In addition, the Bible documents that Jubal was the first person to handle, and one may assume to play, a musical instrument. However, in the Bible, intrinsically linked with music, praise, and worship were the Levites. Let's discuss the role and importance of the Levites within biblical music ministry.

Who Were the Levites?

Levi, meaning attached, was the third son of Jacob and Leah.

She conceived again and bore a son, and said, "Now this time my husband will become attached to me, because I have borne him three sons." Therefore his name was called Levi. (Genesis 29: 34)

Levi and his wife, Melcha, had three sons, Gershon, Kohath, and Merari. From Gershon and Merari's lineage came temple workers, and from Kohath's lineage came the priestly roles. The Gershonites were given the responsibility of moving the tabernacle covers, curtains, screens, and cords with ox carts (Numbers 4: 24–26 and 7: 7–8). The Merarites were principally in charge of moving the tabernacle poles, boards, sockets, pillars, and bars by hand (Numbers 3: 36–37 and 4: 29–33). Finally, the Kohathites had the task of carrying the holy items of the tabernacle. This included carrying the Ark of the Covenant, the lampstand, altars, and utensils with poles. They were responsible for maintaining the work in the holy place both day and night (1 Chronicles 9: 32–33). Furthermore, the priestly lineage began in the tribe of Kohath, with God specifically calling for Aaron and his four sons, who were Kohathites, to serve Him as priests (Exodus 28: 1). Find below a chart of the lineage of Levi.

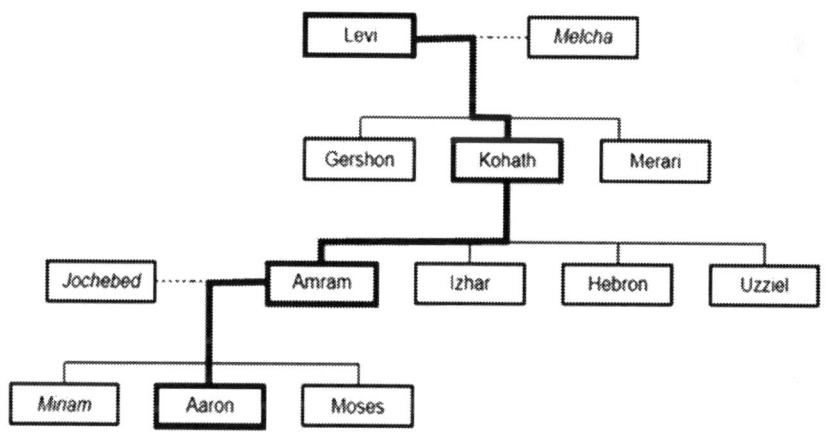

These are the names of the sons of Levi according to their generations: Gershon, Kohath, and Merari. And the years of the life of Levi were one hundred and thirty-seven. And the sons of Kohath were Amram, Izhar, Hebron, and Uzziel. And the years of the life of Kohath were one hundred and thirty-three. Now Amram took for himself Jochebed, his father's sister, as wife; and she bore him Aaron and Moses. And the years of the life of Amram were one hundred and thirty-seven. (Exodus 6: 16, 18, 20)

Reading on, we see in Numbers 3:10 that God commands Moses to exclusively appoint Aaron and his sons as priests. 'So you shall appoint Aaron and his sons that they may keep their priesthood, but the layman who comes near shall be put to death.'

The Role of the Levites

It is said that Yahweh chose the Levites to be in a position of spiritual leadership. To further this, their role was that of a restorer and guardian of true worship to God. They were positioned around the tabernacle where God dwelt, as opposed to joining a particular tribe or camp:

But the Levites shall camp around the tabernacle of the testimony, so that there will be no wrath on the congregation of the sons of Israel. So the Levites shall keep charge of the tabernacle of the testimony. (Numbers 1: 53)

They also guarded the purity of Israel's worship by leading worship (offering the sacrifices in the temple) and by refusing to partake in any pagan worship. The Levites are characterised for having a strong dislike of pagan worship being mixed with the true worship that Yahweh expected from all Israel. This is clearly seen in the story of the Levites killing those who worshipped the golden calf (Exodus 32: 28).

Therefore, in pausing here for a moment, I believe it is fair to say that the modern-day Levite is in fact the worship band (musicians and singers). How many see their role as that of guarding the purity of the worship of the saints? How many would go out on a limb to ensure the removal of all issues that could contaminate the worship of God? How many really see their role as a director of themselves and others in the service of God? If the worship bands were to re-evaluate and minister in accordance to the true purpose of the Levitical role, would this see our churches flourish in the area of worship? As we keep these questions at the forefront of our minds, let's address the true musical role of the biblical Levites.

Any activity in the temple involving the act of worship was exclusively dealt with by the Levite tribe. In fact, the Temple musicians were chosen from any part of the Levite tribe, for example Asaph was a Gershonite (1 Chronicles 6: 39 and 43), Heman was a Kohathite (1 Chronicles 6: 33), and Jeduthun was a Merarite (1 Chronicles 9: 14 and 16). However, it was under King David's rule in Israel that we begin to see the Levite role in music ministry established. When the twelve tribes became settled, David numbered the Levites and introduced some changes, determining they were no more to carry the tabernacle or its items. However, for those aged twenty years and above, they were to support the sons of Aaron doing various duties in the house of the Lord and to worship God through singing every morning and evening (1 Chronicles 23: 26–30). Their involvement became more internal within the tabernacle rather than focusing on the external elements of carrying the tabernacle and ensuring its vessels were safe.

Furthermore, in the Bible records established by David within the music ministry of the tabernacle, the list of names and roles are mentioned (1 Chronicles 25: 1–7).

Although the first time the act of singing mentioned in the Bible is when Miriam celebrates Israel's miraculous deliverance from Egypt via the Red Sea (Exodus 15: 1), note that Heman is the first person recorded with the title of singer within biblical text. In fact, so important became the role of the Levites within the music ministry of the tabernacle that as mentioned earlier, they were 'employed in that work day and night (1 Chronicles 9: 33). Hence, at all times, there was music and singing unto God in the Tabernacle. Imagine that – twenty-four hours of worship, every day of the year! How many churches really pay this much attention to the role of music ministry as a full-time service unto God?

It is presumed that when a person says they are in full-time ministry that we would think of a pastor, an evangelist, or even a missionary. It would be rare to think of a musician; yet, this is exactly what David had established. Further still, there was no discrimination with regards to sex. Both men and women singers were needed and used (Ecclesiastes 2: 8; 2 Chronicles 35: 25; Ezra 2: 65; and Nehemiah 7: 67).

The role of the Levites was not restricted to the house of God. The Bible tells us on a number of occasions that the Levites would also sing and play their instruments in worship to God outside of the house of God (Joshua 6:2 0; 2 Chronicles 20: 21–22; and Nehemiah 7: 1).

In 2 Chronicles 20, we see that Jehoshaphat, the King of Judah, received news that the neighbouring kings had made plans to attack Judah (verse 1 and 2). This terrified him because his army was not as advanced as his enemy's. He called for a nationwide fast and prayed to God for help (verse 3 to 12). God responds via the prophet Jahaziel, 'a Levite of the sons of Aspah' (verse 14). Through Jahaziel, the word came that Jehoshaphat should not be frightened and that he should go down to fight the enemy, God would allow him to be victorious because 'the battle is not yours, but God's' (verse 15). So

Jehoshaphat did as he was instructed, but instead of the army going first with their weaponry, it was the singers who led the way, praising God! This sounds absurd for a leader of a kingdom, who is about to go into battle, to put the worshippers first.

I would strongly suggest that the singers were not just merely singing. As they sang, something was happening to bring defeat to the enemy in a realm that was not physically tangible. I like to call this realm the spiritual realm.

The power of praise and worship cannot be overemphasised, through the singing and worship the victory was won. Jehoshaphat's men did not have to use any physical weapon to fight. By the time they arrived at the enemy's camp, the enemy had turned against one another and killed each another (2 Chronicles 20: 23–24).

Attitude to Worship

Worship is not only about music and singing. According to The Revell Bible Dictionary, worship is defined as 'that attitude and those corporate and personal acts of reverence that are the appropriate response of human beings to God's self-revelation.' From this, we can see that worship has a lot to do with one's attitude. Your attitude is not something you are born with. Rather, it is something developed in your younger years and is developed through your life experiences. It is by this that we are able to form our beliefs and opinions about something or someone, and by extension, we can form a belief and opinion that develops an appropriate attitude to worship.

When looking at the story of the healing of the ten lepers (Luke 17: 11–19), we find that although they were all healed and cleansed, only one had the right attitude and returned to Jesus to thank Him.

This shows us that even after healing and liberation has taken place, worship and giving thanks to God must still continue. In a nutshell, in whatever we are doing, true worship never stops (1 Thessalonians 5: 18).

Preparing the Ground

Let's take a look at how praise and worship can prepare the ground for the presentation of the word of God. What do we mean by the ground?

Do you remember the parable that Jesus gave regarding the ground and the seed (Matthew 13)? Jesus explained that the sower sows the seed and gave the interpretation that the heart represents the ground or soil and that the seed is the word of God. The ground that is prepared to receive seed is called the 'good ground' (verse 23). When the modern-day worship leader leads the congregation into praise and worship, it creates an atmosphere for the congregation members to prepare their hearts (their ground) for the word of God (the seed). This is why it's important for the praise and worship team to sing songs that prepare the people's heart for the message.

To emphasise this point, let us look at 2 Kings 3: 14–15.

And Elisha said, 'As the LORD of hosts lives, before whom I stand, surely were it not that I regard the presence of Jehoshaphat king of Judah, I would not look at you, nor see you. But now bring me a musician.' Then it happened, when the musician played, that the hand of the LORD came upon him.

The prophet Elisha was highly regarded amongst many throughout Israel and Judah. This account records a remarkable story in which the king of Israel (Jehoram) seeks the counsel of Elisha because

Mesha, the king of Moab, waged war against him. Jehoram calls on the help of Jehoshaphat and the king of Edom to join him in allegiance to fight against Mesha. As they go after him, they get lost in the wilderness, with no food or water for themselves or their cattle. In their dilemma, Jehoshaphat asks, 'Is there no prophet of the LORD here, that we may inquire of the LORD by him?' (2 Kings 3: 11). A servant recommends Elisha, and as such, all three kings go to Elisha for help.

Although Elisha does not want to help them, he still agrees to help because of the respect he had for Jehoshaphat, who was a man who knew and recognised God. How does he do this?

Before Elisha seeks God for a word, he calls for a minstrel, who is known to be a skilled musician in praise and worship, to help usher in the presence of God.

It was praise and worship that prepared Elisha's mind and spirit to hear God's voice and direction for these kings. Subsequently, after the worship in song takes place, Elisha was able to let the kings know that they would win the battle because this situation was 'a simple matter in the sight of the LORD; He will also deliver the Moabites into your hand' (2 Kings 3: 18).

Praise and worship also prepares the way for healing.

> And Saul's servants said to him, "Surely, a distressing spirit from God is troubling you. Let our master now command your servants, who are before you, to seek out a man who is a skillful player on the harp. And it shall be that he will play it with his hand when the distressing spirit from God is upon you, and you shall be well." Therefore Saul sent messengers to Jesse,

and said, "Send me your son David, who is with the sheep." And Jesse took a donkey loaded with bread, a skin of wine, and a young goat, and sent them by his son David to Saul. So David came to Saul and stood before him. And he loved him greatly, and he became his armorbearer. Then Saul sent to Jesse, saying, "Please let David stand before me, for he has found favor in my sight." And so it was, whenever the spirit from God was upon Saul, that David would take a harp and play it with his hand. Then Saul would become refreshed and well, and the distressing spirit would depart from him. (1 Samuel 16: 15–16 and 19–23)

Saul, due to disobedience (1 Samuel 16: 1–23), had lost favour with God, and he fell into depression. He could not lift his spirit as before and was in despair. However, his servants recognised the power of music and worship on the human soul, and it is they who called to him that he should seek out a person who had the skill to play the kinnôr (harp). The person chosen was a young shepherd called David, one whom God had chosen to succeed Saul as the King of Israel and also one whom God says is 'a man after my own heart' (Acts 13: 22).

Through his anointed and skilful playing, Saul's depression lifts, and the spirit that was causing Saul distress left him. It is my belief as we are worshipping God, healing is taking place in our very midst, healing of spirit, soul, and body.

How is the Levitical order of music, praise, and worship linked and relevant for today?

Peter, in his first epistle, states that those who believe that Jesus is precious (1 Peter 2: 6–7) are 'a chosen generation, a royal priesthood' (1 Peter 2: 9). In so saying, Peter is explaining that like the priests of old, we now, through Jesus Christ, are called priests. As such, we too have to fulfil our duties in the temple. All those who are in Christ, under the new covenant, are called priests. We may not be Levites by clan or genealogy, but through Christ, we are heirs and children of God and can claim the title of priest.

Paul states that we must present our 'bodies a living sacrifice, holy, acceptable unto God, which is your reasonable service' (Romans 12: 1). Our bodies have become the temple. As such, Jesus' death deemed it unnecessary to present live animals for sacrifice (Hebrews 9: 24–28). Our sacrifice is a symbolic presentation of our own bodies and our praise (Hebrews 13: 15). It can be concluded that based on this explanation, all those who have accepted Christ are in fact modern-day Levites.

Worship Ushers in the Presence of God

In addition, music ministry ushers in the presence of God.

When worship leaders stand at the front of the church and lead the congregation in songs of praise and worship, they are effectively leading a welcome and celebration of God's presence amongst His people. A great example of this is found in 2 Chronicles 5: 11–14 as the worshippers worshipped the very presence of God filled the temple.

> And it came to pass when the priests came out of the
> Most Holy Place (for all the priests who were present
> had sanctified themselves, without keeping to their

divisions), and the Levites who were the singers, all those of Asaph and Heman and Jeduthun, with their sons and their brethren, stood at the east end of the altar, clothed in white linen, having cymbals, stringed instruments and harps, and with them one hundred and twenty priests sounding with trumpets— indeed it came to pass, when the trumpeters and singers were as one, to make one sound to be heard in praising and thanking the LORD, and when they lifted up their voice with the trumpets and cymbals and instruments of music, and praised the LORD, saying: "For He is good, For His mercy endures forever," that the house, the house of the LORD, was filled with a cloud, so that the priests could not continue ministering because of the cloud; for the glory of the LORD filled the house of God. (2 Chronicles 5: 11–14)

This cloud represented the very presence of God. Today, God's presence is represented in the person of the Holy Spirit who represents Him on earth now that Jesus has returned to Him (John 15: 26 and 16: 7). This tells us that those who are in Christ have the Holy Spirit within them and that He represents the very presence of God. As the Ark of the Covenant representing God's presence was in the temple during biblical times, the Holy Spirit now resides in us, as we are God's temple.

I feel it is important to point out that the church is not a building but the people. When Jesus said to Peter, 'on this rock I will build My church, and the gates of Hades shall not prevail against it' (Matthew 16: 18), the rock was symbolic of Peter's confession when he declared that Jesus is the Christ, the Son of the Living God. As was said, the Holy Spirit now dwells within us. As such, this indicates that we are living beings. The church is actually a living and growing organism. When two or three believers come together, they too are called the church, which is why it is important that we understand the power and authority of the church. (Matthew 18: 20).

The Importance of the Role of Song

The Bible tells us clearly that 'iron sharpens iron' (Proverbs 27: 17). This is why it is important that the body of Christ, which is the church, comes together in corporate worship. One of the ways in which we worship is through song. The importance of the role of song is clearly seen here in Colossians 3: 16 when Paul says,

> Let the word of Christ dwell in you richly in all wisdom, teaching and admonishing one another in psalms and hymns and spiritual songs, singing with grace in your hearts to the Lord.

Singing is one of the pinnacles of worship towards God, and it uplifts all who partake of it. Furthermore researchers and psychologists are finding that one of the great therapies for the mind and soul is when a group of likeminded people come together in song. All we have to do is look at and listen to sports fans singing their national anthem or their team's signature song or even a group of people at a concert listening to their favourite pop star. See how the chanting and singing of the songs connect them. They come together as one, unified by a common song. This should be the same in Christendom. Let's be reminded of the instructions in Hebrews 10: 24–25.

> And let us consider one another in order to stir up love and good works, not forsaking the assembling

of ourselves together, as is the manner of some, but exhorting one another, and so much the more as you see the Day approaching.

As the worship leaders, the modern-day Levites lead us in worship, it is important to remember that the primary function of their role is to unite individual hearts. As a worshipper, it is important, before even coming to church, that our hearts and our minds are prepared for united worship. I do not mean to be disrespectful or to trivialise challenges you may have faced, but worship must always be the priority for any worshipper. David encourages us in Psalm 34: 1, 'I will bless the LORD at all times; His praise shall continually be in my mouth.'

When we read Acts 16: 16–26, the situation that Paul and Silas was in was both severe and life-threatening. However, they must have known the benefits of uniting by worshipping in song. Literally at midnight and metaphorically the darkest time of their situation, they decided to worship in song, and it was only when they did this that God performed a miracle.

The Bible states that their chains literally fell off. However, what is intriguing about this story is that the other prisoners' chains fell off too. So this tells us again that worship activates the unseen world (also known as the spiritual realm). In turn, this affects the seen world (also known as the physical realm). Furthermore, the power of worship is so great that it not only affects us but also affects everything around us.

In fact, throughout the Bible, it is clear that worshipping together brings results. This is reiterated by Jesus Himself when He demonstrated that when a kingdom or a house is not united, it will fall (Matthew 12: 25).

Chapter 7

The Tabernacle of the Old Testament

The words 'tabernacle' and 'temple' can be confusing. Let me in a simple way explain the difference. The tabernacle is the English translation of the Hebrew word מִשְׁכָּן 'mishkan,' which simply means residence or dwelling place. According to the Hebrew Bible, this was a portable dwelling place for the presence of God, from the time of the Exodus to the conquering of the promised land (Canaan).

In contrast, the temple is the English translation of the Hebrew word הֵיכָל 'heykal,' meaning a large public building. Unlike the tabernacle, the temple was stationary and also referred to as the palace of Jehovah. It was an elaborately ordained holy place where the people congregated to worship God.

I will focus this chapter on the original tabernacle, which was God's idea, initiative, design, and plan constructed by Moses.

The Tabernacle

Moses built the tabernacle according to the pattern shown to him by God (Exodus 25). In the building of the tabernacle, the people came together in obedience to the word of God given through Moses. I will not go into the specific measurements of the tabernacle, but I will say its total square area was 7,500 square feet. I will explore the three compartments of the tabernacle, the contents within, and the connection between the tabernacle and its relevance to worship in Moses' time as well as how it is symbolic of today's worship.

There are three compartments within the tabernacle. The outer court where the brazen altar and the washbasin are. Through a veiled curtain was the holy place (also known as the inner court), where the menorah, the table of showbread, and the altar of incense were placed. Finally, the Holy of Holies was where the Ark of the Covenant was found.

The Contents of the Outer Court

- Brazen/Brass Altar

As we go through the gate directly in front of us would be the Altar of Burnt Offering (Exodus 27: 1). This is also referred to as the brazen or brass altar. All offerings made by fire took place at this altar. The offering was an innocent animal, without blemish or disease, and there was no way to appease God except for the sacrifices offered on the brazen altar. It was here that sacrifices were made on behalf of the people. The sacrifice was classed as a blood covenant made with Yahweh and actually represented the sinner. It took the sinner's place on the altar.

The Bible refers to shadows, which are prophetic symbols that are to come. It is explained in Hebrews 10: 1 (NLT).

> The old system under the law of Moses was only a shadow, a dim preview of the good things to come, not the good things themselves. The sacrifices under that system were repeated again and again, year after year,

but they were never able to provide perfect cleansing for those who came to worship.

Furthermore, the Bible also explains that:

> If that had been necessary, Christ would have had to die again and again, ever since the world began. But now, once for all time, he has appeared at the end of the age to remove sin by his own death as a sacrifice. (Hebrews 9: 26; NLT)

What was happening in the Old Testament was a shadow of things to come. The real purpose was about Him, Jesus Christ. Jesus became the ultimate sacrifice for the world, and His sacrifice did not have to be repeated. His sacrifice was once and for all. This is clearly detailed in Hebrews 10: 1–10.

So what does this mean for the worshipper today? According to the New Testament, we do not need to bring animal sacrifices, as requested by law, because Jesus is the sacrifice – once and for all. However, God still requires a sacrifice from us. However, it is a sacrifice of praise and thanksgiving. 'Therefore by Him let us continually offer the sacrifice of praise to God, that is, the fruit of our lips, giving thanks to His name.' (Hebrews 13: 15).

But let us consider why Paul says that praising God is a sacrifice. Why does he state that we should do it continually? Furthermore, why is thanksgiving 'the fruit of our lips'?

In the New Testament, the original word 'sacrifice' derives from the Greek word 'thuo', which means 'I sacrifice' (often referring to an animal). What did Paul's statement encouraging us to 'offer sacrifice of praise to God continually' have to do with the original word? To praise God requires a personal sacrifice, and it takes an act of the will to lay our all on the altar before a God we do not understand. When we bring a sacrifice of praise, we choose to believe that even though life is not going as we think it should, God is still good and can be trusted. When we choose to praise God in spite of the storms, He is honoured, and our faith grows deeper.

For example, let us look at the story of when Daniel went through a tough time where the presidents and the princes conspired against him because he was preferred above them. It was said that Daniel was promoted as a president and that Daniel was the top dog. The other presidents and princes became jealous and conspired against him, but they could not find any error or fault in him. They knew the only way to trap him was concerning the law of God. They all conspired against Daniel by bringing a request to King Darius, asking him to make a decree that no one should pray to any god or man for thirty days. If anyone broke this decree, they should be cast into the lion's den (Daniel 6: 7). The president and the princes did this, knowing that if they could convince the king to sign it, they knew they could trap Daniel, a man renowned for prayer and worship.

The king agreed and signed the decree, oblivious to their plan. But Daniel did something amazing! The threat of being in a lion's den did not intimidate him. He obviously made up his mind that he would not cease from his usual prayer and worship times, giving thanks to God.

> Now when Daniel knew that the writing was signed, he went home. And in his upper room, with his windows open toward Jerusalem, he knelt down on his knees three times that day, and prayed and gave

thanks before his God, as was his custom since early
days. (Daniel 6: 10)

When we read the original Hebrew of this verse, it is states that he
did three things:

1. 'He kneeled upon his knees.' The word 'kneeled' is the
   Hebrew word בְּרַךְ 'berek', which derives from the Hebrew
   word בָּרַךְ 'barak', meaning to bend the knees and bow down
   in praise.

2. He prayed. The word 'prayed' is the Hebrew word צְלָה 'tsela',
   which means to bow in prayer.

3. He gave thanks. The word 'thanks' is the Hebrew word יְדָא
   'yeda', meaning to praise, and is derived from Hebrew word
   יָדָה 'yadah', which means praise with extended hands.

Suffice it to say that Daniel was caught praying and thrown into
the lion's den, but God delivered him by sending an angel to shut
the lions' mouths. From that tremendous deliverance, the king was
pleased that Daniel's God delivered him. The King then commanded
that all those who accused and conspired against Daniel to be thrown
into the lion's den with their wives and children. This time, there was
no deliverance for them. Daniel went on to prosper throughout the
whole reign of King Darius.

Daniel is a good role model to show us a pattern of sacrifice of
praise. Our praise to God is not to be based on how we feel or what
situations we face; it is based on who God is. Therefore, real praise
and worship continues regardless of circumstances.

- Laver

Situated between the brazen altar and the holy place is the laver. Otherwise known as the basin, the laver was a bowl made completely of bronze that was filled with water. Before the priests could enter the holy place, it was compulsory for them to wash their hands and feet. They did this under strict instructions from God, via Moses, in order to continue their duties within the Holy Place.

Then the LORD spoke to Moses, saying: "You shall also make a laver of bronze, with its base also of bronze, for washing. You shall put it between the tabernacle of meeting and the altar. And you shall put water in it, for Aaron and his sons shall wash their hands and their feet in water from it. When they go into the tabernacle of meeting, or when they come near the altar to minister, to burn an offering made by fire to the LORD, they shall wash with water, lest they die. So they shall wash their hands and their feet, lest they die. And it shall be a statute forever to them—to him and his descendants throughout their generations. (Exodus 30: 17–21)

The application of this instruction for believers today is that even though we are forgiven through Christ's work on the cross, we are cleansed through the holy Word of God. In order for us to be effective ministers of God, we need to be washed daily by reading and applying His Word to our lives. 'You are already clean

because of the word which I have spoken to you.'
(John 15: 3)

Throughout the scriptures, the word of God has many symbolisms, one of which is that Jesus' word cleanses us once we accept it. That is why when we worship God, a key element of the act of worship is to sing His word, to read His word, and to pray His word. But let's pause here and focus on the act of worship. Singing His word has a dual purpose. Firstly, it brings cleansing to the worshipper.

> Husbands, love your wives, just as Christ also loved the church and gave Himself for her, that He might sanctify and cleanse her with the washing of water by the word, that He might present her to Himself a glorious church, not having spot or wrinkle or any such thing, but that she should be holy and without blemish. (Ephesians 5: 25–27)

Secondly, singing His word invokes the worshipper to draw near to God.

> Let us draw near with a true heart in full assurance of faith, having our hearts sprinkled from an evil conscience and our bodies washed with pure water. (Hebrews 10: 22)

A little note for Christian songwriters – it is imperative that when writing a song, that your focus is on the message of the song. What should this message be? It should be nothing less than the word of God. Remember that no matter how beautiful the melody of the song is, if the message of that song is devoid of God's word, then its desired effect for the listener to be cleansed and be drawn near to

God will not be realised. Instrumentalists, don't feel left out. We will be talking about praising God through musical instruments further on in this book.

Music and the word are not meant to be in conflict with each other. God Himself wants them together, which is why, for example, He tells us in Psalm 147: 1 (NLT), 'Praise the LORD! How good to sing praises to our God! How delightful and how fitting!'

God did not intend that music supersede the Word or that music undermine the Word. Music is to serve the Word. When that relationship is understood and appreciated, music becomes a powerful gift from God that complements, supports, and deepens the impact of the words we sing.

The Contents of the Holy Place

- Shewbread

   On the right side of the holy place is the table of shewbread. Some translations call it the table of showbread. Do not be confused – it is the same thing. It held twelve loaves of bread, which was to represent the twelve tribes of Israel. The priests baked the bread with fine flour, and it remained on the table before the Lord for a week. Every Sabbath day the priests would remove it and eat it in the Holy Place, then it would be replenished every week. Only priests could eat the bread, and it could only be eaten in the holy place as it was holy.

And you shall take fine flour and bake twelve cakes with it. Two-tenths of an ephah shall be in each cake. You shall set them in two rows, six in a row, on the pure gold table before the LORD. And you shall put pure frankincense on each row, that it may be on the bread for a memorial, an offering made by fire to the LORD. Every Sabbath he shall set it in order before the LORD continually, being taken from the children of Israel by an everlasting covenant. And it shall be for Aaron and his sons, and they shall eat it in a holy place; for it is most holy to him from the offerings of the LORD made by fire, by a perpetual statute. (Leviticus 24: 5–9)

In a lot of cases where bread was eaten, it was often at a time of fellowship: 'And they continued steadfastly in the apostles' doctrine and fellowship, in the breaking of bread, and in prayers.' (Acts 2: 42)

If we cast our minds back to the time when the tabernacle was erected, the Bible says that throughout the whole week, the priests would do their duties. They were making sure the menorah was consistently burning and making sure the incense was releasing its perfume continually, and they also carried out the act of sacrificing. This routine continued except for the Sabbath day, when the priests would come together in the holy place to eat the shewbread. Doesn't this seem to resemble an act of fellowship?

In Leviticus 24: 9, when God orders Aaron and his sons (priests) to eat the shewbread together, this must also have been an act of worshipping God.

There are many people who would say that Christians coming together for fellowship and socialising is not for the church. Think again! The priests coming together in fellowship by eating the showbread together took place weekly in the holy place; it was a direct command from God. Also, it is no coincidence that during the time of the Passover, in the New Testament, when Jesus 'took bread, and blessed it, and broke it, and gave it to the disciples, and said, Take, eat; this is My body' (Matthew 26: 26), this was a time of fellowship. They ate and sang together (Matthew 26: 30).

One of the greatest and beautiful things one can see is when a group of believers sit around a table and begin to eat and fellowship together. This is, I hasten to suggest, also an act of worship. It may not be clapping of hands or singing of hymns or even a traditional sermon coming from a pulpit, but this is another aspect of worship that believers tend to overlook.

It is clear to me that the showbread, fellowship, and worship are all intermingled. Every aspect of the tabernacle was designed towards worship, and I am convinced that the act of eating showbread, after sitting on its special table for six days, brought all the priests together to break bread and fellowship together. When we partake in breaking of bread and fellowship together as believers, we are actually worshipping Christ, the bread of life. As we come with a common ground and share in this special meal together, this pleases God.

- Menorah

The menorah was a seven-branched candelabra beaten out of one solid piece of gold that served as one of the sacred vessels in the holy temple. (Each branch is also called a lamp). It stood on the left hand side of the holy place.

The lampstand had a central branch from which three branches extended from each side, forming a total of seven branches. On top of each branch were seven lamps holding olive oil and wicks. Each branch resembled an almond tree, containing buds, blossoms, and flowers. The priests were instructed to keep the lamps burning continuously.

'This is the lampstand that stands in the Tabernacle, in front of the inner curtain that shields the Ark of the Covenant. Aaron must keep the lamps burning in the Lord's presence all night. This is a permanent law for you, and it must be observed from generation to generation. (Leviticus 24: 3, NLT)

The menorah is the sole source of light in the holy place. Without its light, it would have been difficult for the priests to fulfil their role. The light shone on the table of showbread and the altar of incense, and this enabled the priest to fellowship with God and intercede on behalf of God's people. This has got Jesus Christ written all over it! Just as the lampstand was the only source of light in the tabernacle, isn't it ironic that Jesus came into the world as the light of the world and from Him come all other lights, meaning you and me, that follow

Christ (Matthew 5: 14–16)? Jesus, the 'true light that gives light to every man' came into the world so that man could see God and no longer live in spiritual darkness (John 1: 6–13).

Furthermore, Jesus said of Himself that He was the light of the world. Whosoever follows Him will never walk in darkness but will have the Light of life (John 8: 12).

We can clearly see the symbolism of Christ in regards to the menorah, but what does it mean to the worshipper today? From the description of the menorah, other theologians have suggested, and I am in agreement, that the middle branch of the menorah is a symbolic of Jesus and we, as the worshippers (the church) who follow him, are represented by the six branches that extend from the original branch. Paul states, 'and you are complete in Him, who is the head of all principality and power.' (Colossians 2: 10).

However, let's delve a little deeper. In completing my own research, I have discovered the following. There are three main numbers that are highlighted to me: one (the main branch), six (the branches that stem from the main branch), and seven (the main branch and the six branches combined). These numbers are very significant and could also provide us with a better understanding of how the menorah relates to the modern-day worshipper. So let's investigate this further.

- One symbolises unity, primacy, and oneness of the Godhead (Deuteronomy 6: 4; Zechariah 14: 9; and John 10: 30).

- Six symbolises human weakness and the number of mankind as man was created on the sixth day (Genesis 1: 26).

- Seven symbolises both physical and spiritual perfection and completion. Furthermore, creation was completed on the seventh day (Genesis 2: 2).

In analysing this information together, it indicates to me that even in our human weaknesses, the true worshipper must be a representative of Christ, as His branches. In being His branches, we become effective because we are both unified and complete in Him.

Jesus calls us 'light of the world' and commands us to 'In the same way, let your good deeds shine out for all to see, so that everyone will praise your heavenly Father.' (Matthew 5: 16; NLT). But if we look deeper into this, Jesus is saying to the believers that as we shine our light, and we do this by talking about Him, living our life and making sure that all that we say and do is in honour to Him, we will direct the world towards God and cause the onlookers to give God glory. The word for 'praise' in this scripture (in other versions seen as the word 'glory') is the Greek word 'doxazō', which clearly means to extol, magnify, celebrate, praise, impart glory to something, and to cause the dignity and worth of some person or thing to become manifest and acknowledged. Not only do we worship and honour God by shining our light before men, but it also leads others to praise and worship God from whom the source of light comes.

• Altar of Incense

There was a curtain that acted as a partition between the holy place and the Holy of Holies; the altar of incense was placed in front of this. This altar had four horns that projected from its corners; the material it was made from was acacia wood (otherwise known as shittim wood) and was plaited with pure gold (Exodus 30: 1–10).

Twice a day, morning and evening, God ordered the priests to burn incense on the golden altar as they burnt the daily offerings, and this was left burning incessantly as an aroma to please the Lord (Revelation 8: 3–4). Isn't it ironic that Jesus Himself says that we should always pray (Luke 18: 1)? Paul echoes this by saying our prayers should be ceaseless (1 Thessalonians 5: 17).

As ordered by the Lord, the priests mixed four spices, stacte, onycha, galbanum, and pure frankincense. Each portion of spice was equal in quantity. This compound was to be used exclusively within the tabernacle and not for personal use (Exodus 30: 34–38).

Jesus Christ has been declared our intercessor (Hebrews 7: 25). He is declared the High Priest forever after the order of Melchisedec (Hebrews 6: 20). The incense offered on the golden altar represented the prayers of the saints, which only the priests could administer. This act is symbolic of how Christ continually, even to this day, offers prayers to God on our behalf (Romans 8: 34).

It is my belief that prayer is a part of worship. You may ask how is prayer worshipping and praising God. It is important to say that praise and worship should lead us to a deeper consciousness of prayer, and as we pray, there should be a consciousness of worship that leads us into a deeper realm of prayer.

When Jesus taught us how to pray in Matthew 6: 9–13 (The Lord's Prayer), it is important to recognise the model He taught and that he first begins with worship: 'Our Father in heaven, Hallowed be Your name.' This should be the example that we also follow.

Note here that there are obviously other aspects of the Lord's Prayer that are important such as asking God for provision (verse 11), asking God to forgive us whilst we simultaneously forgive others (verse 12), asking God to lead us not into temptation, and asking Him to deliver us from evil (verse 13). This list is not exhaustive. Evidently, you will find that you do pray for other people near and far, and we pray for the sick, people in need, and more.

However, can you imagine if all of us took the Lord's Prayer as it is? Whenever anyone in the world prayed, they prayed that prayer verbatim. This would be a little extreme! I am not saying that we should not use this prayer word for word; I often quote it myself in prayer. What I am saying is that it is my opinion that Jesus was more so providing us with a model for prayer, so that your personal prayer would follow a similar pattern as you pray what is on your heart.

We see that the model that Jesus taught us for prayer ends as it began – with worship: 'For Yours is the kingdom and the power and the glory forever. Amen' (verse 13). As in all things, prayer should begin and end with worship.

The Contents of the Holy Of Holies

• Ark of the Covenant

The Holy of Holies was a room beyond the veil in the holy place where only the High Priest could enter and only once a year, on Yom Kippur (Day of Atonement). On this special day, he would offer sacrifices for himself, his family, and the whole nation of Israel (Leviticus 16: 1–17). But what was inside this special place?

One would imagine an elaborate room with many artefacts. Yet, if we had the privilege of being there, the only furniture we would have seen would be a humble, gold-plated wooden box containing three unlikely items: a jar of bread, a stick budding with flowers, and two stones. If you do not understand the background and purpose for these items, they may seem insignificant until you delve deeper.

The Ark of the Covenant itself was actually a wooden box ornately overlaid, or plated, with gold. On top of the ark were two large cherubim with large wings that met above the ark. The scripture says that God would meet with the High Priest there and speak to him from between the cherubim wings (Exodus 25: 10–22).

Let us look more closely at the three items that were inside the Ark of the Covenant. Firstly, the manna: This was breadlike food provided daily by God for the Israelites when they grumbled during the wanderings in the desert. The people as a memorial kept it – it was literally bread from heaven (Exodus 16: 33).

Jesus compares the manna to Himself and actually states that He came from heaven and He is the true bread. If the children of Israel had manna every day, which kept them for forty years in the wilderness, this tells me that it must have had all the nutrients, vitamins, and energy to sustain them. Jesus states that He is the bread of life that gives life.

> For the bread of God is He who comes down from heaven and gives life to the world." And Jesus said to them, "I am the bread of life. He who comes to Me shall never hunger, and he who believes in Me shall never thirst. Your fathers ate the manna in the wilderness, and are dead. This is the bread which comes down from heaven, that one may eat of it and not die. I am the living bread which came down from heaven. If anyone eats of this bread, he will live forever; and the bread that I shall give is My flesh, which I shall give for the life of the world. (John 6: 33, 35, 49–51)

When looking at the significance and relevance of manna for today's worshipper, it is important to note that the Hebrew word 'manna' מָן means 'what is it?' Today, when talking of Jesus, the bread of life or dare I say the true manna, people are asking who Jesus is and what he is about. However, it is those who partake of him, follow Him, and worship Him who know firsthand of the sustenance and provision He provides physically, spiritually, and emotionally. I believe David rightly captured the essence of what I am explaining when he said, 'Oh, taste and see that the LORD is good; Blessed is the man who trusts in Him!' (Psalm 34: 8).

Secondly, in the Ark of the Covenant is Aaron's rod that had budded. The people, out of jealousy, rebelled against Aaron as their high priest. To resolve the dispute, God commanded the people to take twelve rods labelled with the names of the leader of each tribe and place them before the Ark of the Covenant overnight. The next day, Aaron's rod, from the house of Levi, had budded with blossoms and almonds. God confirmed his choice of Aaron's household as the priestly line (Numbers 17: 1–10).

I believe that this miraculous occurrence took place because God wanted to show Israel that He was not pleased with its lack of faith. Also, He used this phenomenon as a reminder to the people that on more than one occasion, they had rejected God's authority. Furthermore, they had also rejected the leadership of Moses. This was not pleasing to Him.

The budding of Aaron's rod can be likened to the resurrection of Jesus, our eternal God and high priest (John 20: 9 and 1 Corinthians 15: 4). That is to say just as how God used the budding of the rod to confirm Aaron's position and appointment as high priest of Israel, so the resurrection of Jesus Christ is the confirmation that Jesus was the Messiah and eternal high priest.

It is a fact that if Christ had never rose from the dead, then our faith and preaching is pointless (1 Corinthians 15: 14). By this statement, it can also be argued that our praise and worship would be in vain if Christ had not risen from the dead. The reason why we come together in worship, first and foremost, is that Jesus did triumph over death and was raised from the dead. It is not in vain. Every time we come to church to praise, worship, give thanks, and celebrate, let us focus on the fact that Jesus died and rose again. It is this fact that makes our praise and worship real.

Thirdly, the final item inside the Ark of the Covenant is the two stone tablets with the Ten Commandments that God had written with His own finger. In contrast to the first stone tablets that Moses broke, these tablets within the Ark of the Covenant speak to us of the one, the only one, who has ever kept the law of God in its entirety. They speak to us of the one who said, 'Then I said, 'Behold, I have come— In the volume of the book it is written of Me—To do Your will, O God' (Hebrews 10: 7). They are a reminder to us of the importance of obedience, not so much to the law, as we are no longer under the law, but under grace (Romans 6: 14) and to be obedient to God through the love and sacrifice of Jesus.

Please see below a basic layout of the tabernacle.

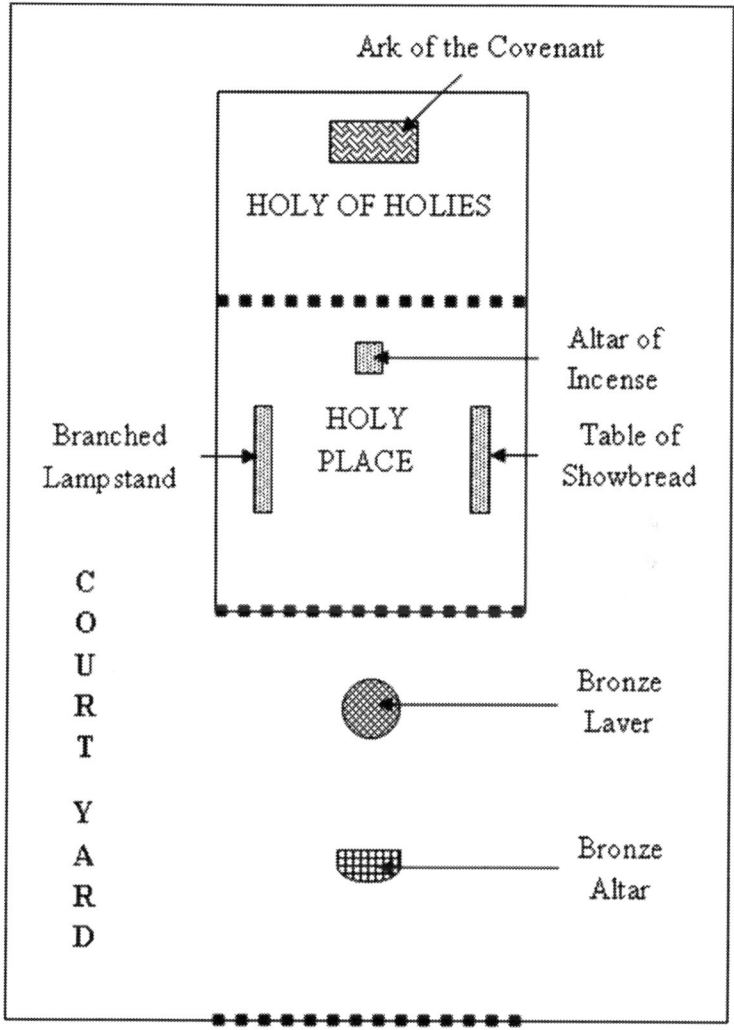

'Enter into His gates with thanksgiving, And into His courts with praise. Be thankful to Him, and bless His name.' (Psalm 100: 4)

Chapter 8

The Temple in the Old Testament

Before we discuss the temple, let's look at the path that led to the temple being constructed.

The tabernacle was a portable tent used to worship God, as explained in the previous chapter. The temple is where the Ark of Covenant was placed; however, the temple was a permanent setting

Moses and his successor Joshua had died Approximately 380 years later, we come to David. The Bible explains that King David was a man after God's own heart (1 Samuel 13: 13–14 and Acts 13: 22). David regularly entered the house of the Lord (i.e., the tabernacle set up under Moses) to worship Yahweh (2 Samuel 12: 20 and Psalm 122: 1). David too was a worshipper; he enjoyed spending time in worship to God. When he was grieving, he went to worship God When he was successful, he went to worship God. Even when things did not go his own way, he went to worship God.

One day, as King David was looking from his palace, he spoke to Nathan the prophet, and he said, 'See now, I dwell in a house of cedar, but the ark of the covenant of the LORD is under tent curtains, Then Nathan said to David, "Do all that is in your heart, for God is with you."' (1 Chronicles 17: 1–2).

This is clear that David had in his heart to build and erect a new permanent tabernacle for the worship of God. This was later to be called the temple.

However, King David was a mighty warrior of God who was known to have engaged in many wars defending Israel and its heritage, albeit under the direction of God. It was because of this that God spoke to David, saying he would not build the temple because he had shed too much blood in God's sight (2 Samuel 7: 8–17 and 1 Chronicles 22: 6–10). It was David's son Solomon who built the temple, but we will look at this later.

In the interim, before Solomon had built the temple, the children of Israel's enemies, the Philistines, had waged war on them and stolen the Ark of the Covenant. The Ark of the Covenant was the most precious thing Israel had; in fact, it represented the very presence of God. What exactly happened to the Ark of the Covenant when it was captured, and what is this going to teach us about worship?

Dagon's Temple

The Ark of the Covenant was taken to the temple of Dagon. Dagon was the chief deity of the Philistines. He was a graven image, half-man and half-fish. There are three places where Dagon is mentioned in the Bible. The first time is in Judges 16: 23 where we are told that Dagon was the god of the Philistines. The second time is in 1 Samuel 5, where the true God, Yahweh, brings Dagon to humiliation, which we'll look at shortly. Finally, in 1 Chronicles 10: 10, in a temple of Dagon, the head of King Saul was fastened.

Going back to 1 Samuel 5, you will see the Philistines had captured the Ark of the Covenant and that they carried it into Dagon's temple and set it beside Dagon. However, early the next morning, when they went into the Temple, there was Dagon, having fallen on his face on the ground before the ark of the Lord! They took Dagon and put him back in his place, but when they returned to Dagon's temple once again the following morning, the idol was on his face on the ground before the ark of the Lord. This time, his head and hands had broken off and were lying on the floor; only his body remained. The Bible states in 1 Samuel 5: 5 that unto this day neither the priests of Dagon nor any other person who entered Dagon's temple in the city of Ashdod walked on the area of the floor where he fell.

After this event, the people of the city of Ashdod were very afraid. The Bible also goes on to say that Yahweh struck down the people of Ashdod with boils, and it was at that point that the people of the city of Ashdod said, 'The ark of the God of Israel must not remain with us, for His hand is harsh toward us and Dagon our god.' (1 Samuel 5: 7).

The Bible says the things that were written beforehand were given as an example for us to learn from (Romans 15: 4). As such, 1 Samuel 5 teaches us today that God does not want us to mix our worship with other gods (Exodus 20: 4–5).

Throughout the Bible, it clearly teaches us that we are to turn away from idolatry (1 Corinthians 10: 14 and 1 John 5: 21), meaning the worshipping of anything or any person who is not God the creator (Romans 1:25). I am not saying we should not respect people. However, there should be a clear distinction of whom we are worshipping; we cannot worship God and other things (Matthew 6: 24). We are to worship only Yahweh, the creator (Revelation 19: 10 and Revelation 22: 9).

Worship is an innate act for human beings, whether we recognise this or not. We as human beings were created to worship God. If we do not worship God and put Him in His rightful place, there will be a void that we will feel compelled to fill. Thus, if it is not God we are worshipping, one way or another, we will worship something or someone else. The reality is that everything else we worship will not give us the fulfilment that we need. That fulfilment comes only when we worship the true God completely in spirit and in truth.

At this point, let us reflect on Elijah's profound statement in 1 Kings 18: 21:

> And Elijah came to all the people, and said, "How long will you falter between two opinions? If the LORD is God, follow Him; but if Baal, follow him." But the people answered him not a word.

Ark of the Covenant Returned

After the Philistines had returned the Ark of the Covenant, King David and his army attempted to transport it back home by way of a cart. However, the oxen pulling the cart stumbled and the ark begins to fall. Uzzah, one of King David's men, instinctively reached out to steady the ark, but unfortunately, this act resulted in his death. He had inappropriately touched a holy item (2 Samuel 6: 3–8 and 1 Chronicles 13: 7–10). In order to appease God and to avoid any more deaths, King David had the ark moved to the Levite Obed-Edom's house. It stayed there for another three months (2 Samuel 6: 9–11). After this time had passed, King David eventually makes a second attempt to relocate the ark. This time, though, he wanted to follow the correct procedure of transporting the ark in accordance to God's directive given to Moses:

> And the children of the Levites bore the ark of
> God on their shoulders, by its poles, as Moses had
> commanded according to the word of the LORD (1
> Chronicles 15: 15)

To fully prepare to return the Ark to its rightful place, David calls all the priests (the Levites) together and instructs them to ceremonially prepare themselves. Furthermore, David assembles a ceremonial marching band, with singers and instruments, to accompany the ark from Gath to Jerusalem (1 Chronicles 15: 3 and 12–16). Amidst the music and celebration, David danced with joy before the Ark of the Covenant (2 Samuel 6: 14). King David danced? Yes, he did, and there is much controversy surrounding the topic of dance within the modern church. Should it be a part of worship? Let's take a close look at this subject.

Dance

In the New Testament, there are two Greek words that mean 'to dance'. The first word is 'orchemai' ὀρχέομαι (Mark 6: 22), and the second word is 'choros' χορός (Luke 15: 25). Both were traditional forms of dance. In fact, in the Hebrew tongue, it is called the Horah, and this is usually performed to Jewish songs. This dance is usually started by everybody forming a circle, holding hands or interlocking arms, and then moving together in a circular motion. Needless to say, this is usually a cheerful and celebrative occasion.

However, there are two other Greek words that I want to look at that I believe could easily be translated for 'dance'. These are 'agalliao' (Luke 10: 21) and 'hallomai' (Acts 3: 8). Let me explain why I have come to this conclusion. It was during my research I found that both these Greek words were directly linked to two Hebrew words for 'dance' in the account of the returning of the Ark of the Covenant in 2 Samuel 6:14.

When we look at the word 'danced' in 2 Samuel 6: 14, we see that it is the Hebrew word 'karar' כָּרַר, which means to whirl, to dance, or to exult. However, it's interesting to note in the parallel account of this event in 1 Chronicles 15: 29 that the Hebrew word for 'dancing' is 'raqad' רָקַד, which means to stamp, spring about wildly, dance, jump, leap, or skip. In effect, we get an even clearer picture of the expression of King David's actions when we combine the two words used to describe the very same act. David didn't just dance; the scripture here suggests he danced wildly!

This really caught my attention; I wanted to explore the reasons as to why two different words were used for dance at the same event.

My explorations had taken me to Luke 10: 21, where Jesus prayed a prayer of thanksgiving:

> In that hour Jesus rejoiced in the Spirit and said, "I thank You, Father, Lord of heaven and earth, that You have hidden these things from the wise and prudent and revealed them to babes. Even so, Father, for so it seemed good in Your sight.

Note the word 'rejoiced' is 'agalliao' ἀγαλλιάω in Greek, which means to rejoice, to exult, be exceeding glad, and greatly rejoice. This is nothing unusual on the surface, but as I looked deeper, I discovered that the Greek word 'agalliao' actually derives from two Greek words. The first is 'agan', which means much, and the second is 'hallomai' ἅλλομαι, which means leaping, springing, or gushing up. In effect, Luke was saying that Jesus was doing much leaping in the spirit! This sheds a new light on how we view Jesus' actions in this part of the scripture.

Further still, during my research I also looked at Acts 3: 8: 'So he, leaping up, stood and walked and entered the temple with them—walking, leaping, and praising God.'

I found that the Greek word for leaping in the last part of this verse is the Greek word 'hallomai' ἅλλομαι, which as explained earlier means to leap, jump, spring up, or gush up. The primitive root is 'hal', which literally means to leap. Further still, the Greek word 'hallomai' is equivalent to the Latin word 'salio', which means to leap and dance. When looking at these different words, we can see that they are directly or indirectly linked to a form of dancing.

When we go back to look at how David danced in 1 Chronicles 15: 29, the word 'raqad' according to the LXX (Septuagint), is actually translated as orcheomai, which, as mentioned earlier, means to dance. Putting all these words together, it can be argued that the Greek words 'hallomai', 'agalloai', and 'orcheomai' are the equivalent to the Hebrew words 'raqad' and 'karar' and are closely connected by definition. I believe these words refer to a spontaneous act of dance and celebration.

Is it a possibility when the Bible states that Jesus rejoiced (agalliao) in spirit that He was actually doing much dancing and celebrating just like King David in 2 Samuel 6: 14? Furthermore, could it be possible that when the Bible states the lame man at Gate Beautiful leaped (hallomai) that he actually danced and praised the Lord? As a side note, it is interesting to point out that the definition of the English word 'dance' is also to leap, jump, or spring.

I have heard it often said that dancing within worship/church should not be allowed; however, I would beg to differ. First of all, the Bible states in 1 Corinthians 14: 40 that everything should be done decently and in order. This would indicate to me that there is nothing wrong with worshipping God through dance as long as it is in line with 1 Corinthians 14: 40. Second, praise and worship can be quiet and reflective, and often, it can be upbeat and exuberant. I believe that dance can be used to present the various types of praise and worship to God without being out of order.

When we think about what God has done for us through Jesus Christ, it can cause us to dance and rejoice. Should we really tell somebody who has experienced something miraculous through God that he should not be dancing in worship? I think not! If we use words to express how we feel towards God, then why can we not through dance and movement or indeed any other form of art?

Also, I have heard that praise and worship should not involve feelings because feelings are subject to change on a daily basis. Saying all of that, it is imperative to remember that praise is based on what God has done. Worship is based on who God is. Furthermore, God is a God of compassion and mercy, and the Bible states that Jesus can be touched with the feelings of our infirmities (Hebrews 4: 15). The word 'infirmities' in this scripture means a weakness or a sickness or a disease of the mind or body. So therefore, we ought to praise and worship God, even through our infirmities.

It is said that true worship is how we feel with our emotions. However, it can become superficial if we base our worship on our emotions alone, as emotive feelings are susceptible to change. Yet, it is my opinion that part of true worship does involve feelings with our heart and emotion, but the greater aspect of worship is to worship with our spirit. I come to this conclusion because Jesus said that 'God is Spirit, and those who worship Him must worship in spirit and truth' (John 4: 24). When we look at the Greek word 'spirit' pneuma, its core meaning refers to the rational spirit, the power by which a human being feels, thinks, and decides. Nonetheless, this must be balanced with the last part of Jesus' statement, 'in truth' the Greek word, *alētheia*, of which one of its key definitions is to look objectively at the reality and truth of a matter.

Therefore, I believe if one desires to praise and worship God through movement and dance, as David did, then why should this be stopped? Although Michal, David's wife, did not approve of his dancing, God did not object! God objected to many things, but He did not object to David dancing. Surely, this alone speaks volumes to us as modern-day worshippers.

As well as exuberant dance, David also organises an impromptu, fully functional musical marching ensemble, which included musicians playing their musical instruments and singers from the Levite community. Based on this, it could be apparent that the Levites had a system in place, whether musical notation that gave structure to their playing and singing together and/or a structure in place for them to be able to play together on short notice. Could this have involved practising together as singers and musicians? I would conclude most definitely!

Chapter 9

Music and the Temple

Musical Instruments

It is important to note that when Moses was given the original instructions, in Numbers 4, of how the holy items were to be transported, music was not part of the plan. Furthermore, it does not state in 2 Samuel 6 that God had commanded David to establish music and singing when the ark was being returned. Some might say that assembling a musical ensemble was a risky instruction given by David considering what had happened to Uzzah (2 Samuel 6: 7). Nevertheless, when we go to the account of King Hezekiah restoring the temple in 2 Chronicles 29: 25–30, we see that King Hezekiah reinstated the musicians in the house because it was a command that came directly from God to King David.

> And he stationed the Levites in the house of the LORD with cymbals, with stringed instruments, and with harps, according to the commandment of David, of Gad the king's seer, and of Nathan the prophet; for thus was the commandment of the LORD by His prophets. (2 Chronicles 29: 25)

So we can deduce that King David did not establish the musical ensemble because he liked music or because he felt like it. Rather, it was done as a result of a direct command from Yahweh.

Further still, the book of Isaiah records a poem Hezekiah wrote after being healed by God from a terminal illness. In it, he makes reference to singing always in the house of God: 'The LORD was ready to save me; Therefore we will sing my songs with stringed instruments All the days of our life, in the house of the LORD.' (Isaiah 38: 20).

However, it may surprise some to know that today, there are many individuals and denominations that say that there should be no musical instruments in church. One of the reasons for this ideology is that even though music is mentioned frequently throughout the Old Testament, in the New Testament, there is no mention of musical instruments being played in the temple for worship. If we look at the surface of this belief, we conclude that it is true that there is no reference and authority given in the New Testament for the playing of musical instruments in the temple. In fact, every time the word 'music' is mentioned in the New Testament, it is in reference only to singing (using the voice as an instrument). One such scripture is Ephesians 5:19: 'speaking to one another in psalms and hymns and spiritual songs, singing and making melody in your heart to the Lord.'

In this verse, though, the word 'melody' is the Greek word '*psallō*' ψάλλω, which means to touch, to pluck, and to play on a stringed instrument. Hence, researchers argue that the phrase 'in your heart' could imply it is referring to something, which is internal, not a physical instrument.

For all those who feel that a musical instrument cannot be used in church for praise and worship, let me share with you some research I have found on this topic. I believe it is down to personal choice. Whether you worship with or without musical instruments, I personally do not believe that it matters to God, as long as praise and worship is done unto the Lord (Colossians 3: 23–24).

In Psalm 19: 4 it states, 'Their line has gone out through all the earth, And their words to the end of the world. In them He has set a tabernacle for the sun.'

One of the literal meanings of the word 'line' in this scripture is a 'musical string'. Paul actually quotes from this verse in Romans 10: 18, where he states, 'But I say, have they not heard? Yes indeed: "Their sound has gone out to all the earth, And their words to the ends of the world." In this verse, the word 'sound' is equivalent to the word 'line' in Psalm 19: 4. Its literal meaning is musical sound. Both words refer to a musical note, but why did Paul specifically refer to sound and words. I believe he wanted to make it clear that it is not just words that go out. A musical sound also goes out.

Remember that it was God who commanded King David to position the musicians in the tabernacle (2 Chronicles 29: 25). Also, there was an important prophecy in Amos 9: 11 referring to the legacy of David, which states:

> On that day I will raise up The tabernacle of David,
> which has fallen down, And repair its damages; I will
> raise up its ruins, And rebuild it as in the days of old;

I believe that this prophecy is relevant for now. When I say now, I mean for this dispensation of grace. It was King David who set up the singing and musical instruments within the tabernacle, and it was no mistake when Amos prophesied that it was David's tabernacle that would be built again by God Himself.

In Acts 15: 16, James quotes this same prophecy of Amos. Interestingly, when James refers to Amos' prophecy, he was in the midst of a dispute about circumcision. In Acts 15, there was a heated discussion between the leaders regarding the question of Gentiles being circumcised. Peter rose and said, and I paraphrase, that there's no longer a need for circumcision as it was a yoke upon people's necks that they frankly could not bear. However, everyone should believe that through the grace of the Lord Jesus Christ they shall be saved, even the Gentiles (Acts 15: 10–11). (Paul agrees with this point in Galatians 5: 6).

With this in mind, we can argue that Amos' prophecy, which was quoted by James, still stands as there is nowhere in the New Testament that God was opposed to musical instruments in worship. I conclude that if God wanted to stop worship through music in the temple, He would have given clear instructions to the New Testament apostles, just as He did on the subject of circumcision, as music is something that is close to His heart.

It is my belief that there is a place for musical instruments in praise and worship within the church, but if you so desire to worship without musical instruments, that is fine too.

Materials of Praise

I am a firm believer that every word in the Bible has significance and deep spiritual meaning that God, by His Holy Spirit, wants us to be aware of. So there are no coincidences. That's why studying the Holy Bible and/or reading biblical study material is important for a Christian's spiritual growth. The Bible states, 'Be diligent to present yourself approved to God, a worker who does not need to be ashamed, rightly dividing the word of truth' (2 Timothy 2: 15). Although the Bible was written by human hands, it is God-breathed; in other words, the Bible was inspired by God (2 Timothy 3: 16).

As such, the Bible mentions that musical instruments were made from two types of wood: the fir tree (2 Samuel 6: 5) and the Almug tree (1 Kings 10: 12). Keeping in mind that the Bible has significance and meaning and there are no coincidences but rather God-incidences, let's look at what the Bible tells us about these two trees.

Before I discuss the fir tree, also known as the fir wood, let me briefly mention and explain about a theory called the Law of First Mention.

Whenever a word or words are first mentioned in the Bible, it is often a keystone to the significance and meaning to that word. This is the Law of First Mention. So bearing this in mind, let's look at the fir wood in more detail. Its first mention in the Bible is in 2 Samuel 6: 5 and it states:

> Then David and all the house of Israel played music before the LORD on all kinds of instruments of fir wood, on harps, on stringed instruments, on tambourines, on sistrums, and on cymbals.

In verse one of the same chapter, King David chooses 30,000 men to accompany him as he returns the Ark of the Covenant to its rightful place. As you can imagine, this was going to be a great celebration. The Ark of the Covenant, representing the very presence of God, was coming back. Sadness would be turned into celebration of praise and joy. David could have chosen to use any type of wood to make the instruments of praise; however, he specifically chose the fir tree/fir wood. I believe that it can be said that he chose this specific wood as it symbolised and was associated with celebration, joy, praise, and worship. As such, it aptly served the right mood in which the Ark of the Covenant was returned, surrounded by musical instruments made of fir wood. No wonder David danced upon hearing the sound produced by these musical instruments. Also, Isaiah 55: 12–13 says:

> For you will go out with joy And be led forth with peace; The mountains and the hills will break forth into shouts of joy before you, And all the trees of the field will clap their hands. "Instead of the thorn bush the cypress will come up, And instead of the nettle the myrtle will come up, And it will be a memorial to the LORD, For an everlasting sign which will not be cut off.

It's important to note here that fir wood and cypress is the same Hebrew word 'berowsh'. 'For you shall go out with joy ...' and 'instead of the thorn bush the cypress will come up': Doesn't that sound like praise, joy, and blessings?

I feel it imperative here to refer back to the Law of the First Mention and look at the word 'thorns'. The first time it is mentioned in the Bible is in the story of the Garden of Eden (Genesis 3: 18). After Adam and Eve disobeyed God and ate from the tree of the knowledge of good and evil, God gave specific punishments, one of which was that He cursed the ground and caused thorns to grow from it. From that time on, throughout the Bible, thorns symbolised a type of curse. To further emphasise this point, we only have to look at Jesus' trial when the soldiers mocked him by making him wear a crown of thorns. However, even though the thorns, a symbol of the curse, were placed on Jesus' head (Matthew 26: 29) (and indeed the Bible said He became the curse for us [Galatians 3: 13]), He, being the Lion of the Tribe of Judah (Judah meaning praise), was victorious over the curse by His death and resurrection!

In light of what I have explained, Isaiah's words are prophetic and an example of why we are to praise God. Indeed, instead of the thorn (the curse), God caused the fir tree (joy and celebration) to come up. He turned the curse into joy and blessings. This is why we praise God!

The second place mentioning how musical instruments were made is in 1 Kings 10: 12 and 2 Chronicles 9: 11. Here, the scripture says the instruments were made of almug wood. This is the first mention of almug trees, and you will note that like the fir tree, the first mention is made with reference to the making of musical instruments:

> the king made steps of the almug wood for the house of the LORD and for the king's house, also harps and stringed instruments for singers. There never again came such almug wood, nor has the like been seen to this day. (1 Kings 10: 12)

The fact that the almug tree was used to make musical instruments of praise and celebration is proof of the fact that it was in the same category as the fir tree. Also, the fact that the almug wood was used both in the king's palace and the temple is a clear approval by God of its use.

Out of all the materials of the earth, it can be argued that stones are the least of the hierarchy chain. Yet, Jesus states that if mankind ceases to worship God, the stones will cry out (Luke 19: 40).

God's creation was music to His ears. After creation, the Bible records that six times God looked at the work of His hands and said it was good. After the seventh time, He said it was very good (Genesis 1: 4, 10, 12, 18, 21, 25, and 31). He was pleased with what He had accomplished as everything He had created was perfect and fit for purpose. Nevertheless, not only did each thing created fulfil a practical purpose, but also a spiritual purpose to praise and worship its Creator in its own way. How amazing is this! In fact, we know there are things in nature that God created to communicate praises to Him. They were created with the ability to emanate a sound in an organised fashion. This sound is a sound of praise perceptible at least to God Himself.

The Bible tells us on many occasions that nature praises God. How do we know this? Well, David states in his song of praise that 'Then the trees of the forest will sing for joy before the LORD; For He is coming to judge the earth.' (1 Chronicles 16: 33; NLT).

In addition, the prophet Isaiah says,

> Sing, O heavens, for the LORD has done it! Shout, you lower parts of the earth; Break forth into singing, you mountains, O forest, and every tree in it! For the LORD has redeemed Jacob, And glorified Himself in Israel. (Isaiah 44: 23)

> For you shall go out with joy, And be led out with peace; The mountains and the hills Shall break forth

into singing before you, And all the trees of the field shall clap their hands. (Isaiah 55: 12).

The Bible also says that God asks Job to answer a list of questions; however, it was evident that Job had no answer for these questions. Here, though, we see that God said the stars sang, again proving that nature praises God, 'To what were its foundations fastened? Or who laid its cornerstone, When the morning stars sang together, And all the sons of God shouted for joy?' (Job 38: 6–7) The root word here for 'sang' is to shout with joy and rejoice.

Furthermore, the other natural music would be that of the animals. King Solomon says, 'The flowers appear on the earth; The time of singing has come, And the voice of the turtledove Is heard in our land.' (Song of Solomon 2: 12).

Solomon's Temple and the Presence of God

As mentioned before, King David did not build the temple, although he did provide gold for its construction (1 Chronicles 29: 2). King Solomon, David's son, was commissioned with the task of building the temple. It took him seven years to complete it, and what a magnificent sight it was. It was the talk of the world! The Bible records how the Queen of Sheba came with copious gifts for Solomon after hearing about the great work he had done. She saw the grandness of his work and even went to the Temple with him, watching him present his offerings and worship to God (1 Kings 10: 5).

After King Solomon had completed building the temple, he preached a sermon to the people of Israel who had gathered at the temple. He reminded the people of the word God gave to his father, King David, saying,

> Nevertheless you shall not build the temple, but your
> son who will come from your body, he shall build the
> temple for My name. (2 Chronicles 6: 9)

After his sermon, Solomon then stood before the altar, worshiped, and said an intercessory prayer to God, asking Him to bless, keep, and protect all those who turn to the temple in prayer (2 Chronicles 6: 12–42). Can you imagine what a solemn and gracious occasion this was? It must have been one of those once-in-a-lifetime moments.

The Dedication of the Temple

So after the prayer, the Bible tells of the grand dedication of the temple (2 Chronicles 7: 1–6). Let us take a closer look at the account, verse by verse.

> When Solomon had finished praying, fire came down
> from heaven and consumed the burnt offering and the
> sacrifices; and the glory of the LORD filled the temple.
> (2 Chronicles 7: 1)

After Solomon ended his prayer, the fire came down from heaven and consumed the burnt offering and sacrifices. What does that mean? A similar event of fire and glory coming down from heaven took place at the time of Moses and Aaron. Look at these verses.

> And Moses and Aaron went into the tabernacle of
> meeting, and came out and blessed the people. Then
> the glory of the LORD appeared to all the people, and
> fire came out from before the LORD and consumed
> the burnt offering and the fat on the altar. When all

the people saw it, they shouted and fell on their faces
(Leviticus 9: 23–24)

This occurred quite a few times throughout the Old Testament
(for example, God consumes Elijah's sacrifice [1 Kings 18: 38] and
God also accepts and consumes David's sacrifice [1 Chronicles 21:
26]). It is often the case that whenever God accepted a sacrifice, He
displayed His approval by sending fire to consume the sacrifice.

So the fact that the fire fell from heaven and consumed Solomon's
sacrifice, we can construe that God was demonstrating His acceptance
of the sacrifices offered. Accompanying His acceptance by fire, the
Bible then states in the first and second verse a weighty statement,
' …and the glory of the LORD filled the temple.'

What is the glory of the Lord? The Hebrew word for glory is
'kabod' כָּבוֹד, and its original meaning is weight or heaviness. The
same word is then used to express importance, honour, and majesty.
Furthermore, it is also to be interpreted as the very character of God
Himself.

Often, Christians will say the words 'shekinah glory' when
referring to the glory of God. However, it is important to mention
that the word 'shekinah' does not in itself appear in the English or
Hebrew translation of the Bible. Shekinah is derived from the Hebrew
verb 'shakan' שכן, which means to settle, inhabit, or dwell (Exodus
40: 35 and Isaiah 57: 15).

Interestingly, the Hebrew word for the tabernacle is mishkan,
which is also a derivative of shakan, and is used in the sense of the
dwelling place of God on earth in the Bible (Psalm 132: 5). As such,
we can infer that the Shekinah glory refers to God Himself coming
to dwell with His people. As we return to 2 Chronicles 7, we read:

And the priests could not enter the house of the LORD, because the glory of the LORD had filled the LORD's house. When all the children of Israel saw how the fire came down, and the glory of the LORD on the temple, they bowed their faces to the ground on the pavement, and worshiped and praised the LORD, saying: "For He is good, For His mercy endures forever. (2 Chronicles 7: 2–3)

The presence of God was manifested in such a way that the priests could not enter into the temple. The children of Israel worshipped and praised the Lord. The word 'worshipped' here is the Hebrew word 'shachah' שָׁחָה, meaning to bow down and to prostrate oneself. The word 'praised' is the Hebrew word 'yadah' יָדָה, meaning to praise with open hands. Whichever way we interpret this, we could not fail to miss how magnificent this occasion was.

You may ask if the Shekinah glory manifests itself today? In my opinion, I say a definite yes, but not in the same way it did in the Old Testament. Let me explain. The Bible says, 'And the Word became flesh and dwelt among us' (John 1: 14).

The phrase 'the Word became flesh' here is referring to Jesus Christ becoming man. The word 'dwelt' in this scripture is the Greek word 'skenoo', which means to tabernacle or to dwell. It is the equivalent to the Hebrew word 'mishkan'. The Bible tells us in Exodus 25: 22 that God's very presence overshadows the two cherubim above the mercy seat of the Ark of the Covenant. It is the place where He will meet with man. The New Testament confirms this by saying the glory (the presence of God) was above the mercy seat in the tabernacle (Hebrews 9: 5).

From the very offset, John tells us of the deity of Christ. I believe that Jesus, the word of God that tabernacles with us, was and remains the glory that was seen in the tabernacle and the temple. This Jesus Christ, who dwelt with the people of the New Testament, is the same God of the Old Testament. Furthermore, Jesus still dwells with us today in the person of the Holy Spirit (Matthew 1: 23; Matthew 28: 20; and 1 John 4: 13) and lives amongst and within us. No wonder Paul says to let us come boldly before the throne of grace where we can obtain mercy (Hebrews 4: 16).

Finally, I want to look at 2 Chronicles 7: 6 (NLT):

> The priests took their assigned positions, and so did the Levites who were singing, "His faithful love endures forever!" They accompanied the singing with music from the instruments King David had made for praising the Lord. Across from the Levites, the priests blew the trumpets, while all Israel stood.

Can you imagine what a glorious time this would have been? Music, praise, and worship were taking place simultaneously unto God. However, I want to pick up on the last section of this verse: 'the priests blew the trumpets … all Israel stood.' The question we need to ask is why the Bible differentiated the musicians from the trumpeters. For this, we need to go back to Numbers 10: 1–10.

As referred to in the first chapter of this book, the trumpet was used for various things, such as the assembly of all Israel to the entrance of the tabernacle and the assembly of the leaders and to indicate a time of praise.

When we look at the original Hebrew word for 'blew the trumpets' in 2 Chronicles 7: 6, we find the word 'chatsar' חָצַר. This word literally means to sound a trumpet playing on or sound with clarions. The word 'clarion' ultimately derives from the Latin word 'clario', meaning clear, to clarify, clarity, to signify, to declare, or to make clearly known. This tells us that it was imperative that the priest who blew the trumpet had to be precise and clear in what he wanted the sound to signify. What's more is the fact that after the priests blew the trumpet and all Israel stood means that the priest did use the trumpet call to give a clear signal. Just imagine the confusion if he had not been clear!

No wonder Paul says in 1 Corinthians 14: 8–9,

> For if the trumpet makes an uncertain sound, who will prepare for battle? So likewise you, unless you utter by the tongue words easy to understand, how will it be known what is spoken? For you will be speaking into the air.

If the message is not clear, then the people cannot follow suit. Stand up!

Interestingly, the trumpet belongs to the wind instruments, and by nature of its group name, the trumpet is one of the only groups of instruments in the Bible that produces a musical note by use of air blown into it. It is significant to recognise that the Holy Spirit's name, both in Hebrew (רוּחַ ruach) and Greek (πνεῦμα pneuma), means air or wind.

So for the relevancy of today's worship leader or any other leader, just as how the priests in 2 Chronicles 7: 6 took their place, today's worship leaders should also take their place in preparation to worship.

If we look at how the priests and leaders prepared themselves to minister, although it was strenuous, it was a command by God that they had to follow. This preparation included such things as washing themselves with water (Exodus 29: 4). The modern-day worship leader must do the same before he or she comes before the congregation. How must we wash ourselves today? Now, I'm not talking about soap and water! We wash ourselves by applying the word of God (Ephesians 5: 26 and John 15: 3). To read the Bible daily is a must!

Another command of preparation that the Old Testament priests had to follow was to be clothed in their priestly garments (Exodus 29: 9). Today, the worship leader and worshipper is called to be clothed with the garments of praise (Isaiah 61: 3). Furthermore, we are to be clothed with Christ and His righteousness (Romans 13: 14 and Luke 24: 49). The phrase 'put on' in Romans 13: 14 is the Greek word ἐνδύω 'endyō', which literally means put on clothes. So the Bible is calling us to literally be clothed with Christ; this is what makes us priests.

Finally, God commands the priests to present a bull to be offered as a sin offering (Exodus 29: 10–14). It is imperative that before the worship leader comes before the congregation that any sin is acknowledged and confessed before God (1 John 1: 9). Hence, when you stand before God's people to lead them into worship, know that you do not stand in your own righteousness. Rather, you stand clothed in Christ's righteousness, and you are free from sin (2 Corinthians 5: 21). Don't forget to always pray for yourselves and one another, and if you have hurt anyone, clear the air (James 5: 16).

The physical preparation is also important; it involves practise, fellowship, and practise. Many Christians and worship leaders may feel confident in their own ability and talents; they may feel that they do not need to put in the amount of practise that those who are less confident do. However, some of the best singers in the world still have singing lessons and still practise. A dedicated worship leader will make sure that he or she is involved in maintaining their ability.

Finally, having the right motivation will always allow the anointing to flow freely. What do I mean? Well, just because you have great talent and ability in music does not give you the right to skip practise or avoid spending time in fellowship with those you minister with. Yes, the anointing is important! After all, the Hebrew word for anointing literally means to smear or rub with oil, so being anointed of God means that God rubs Himself on you to empower you for service. Jesus Himself was anointed, and He still took time out to pray and to fellowship (Luke 4: 18 and Acts 10: 38). Yes, having natural ability and talents are great! But remember it is God who will reward us according to our works (1 Corinthians 3: 12–15). Whatever you do, do not be motivated by seeking the approval of others but rather be motivated by seeking the approval of God (Matthew 6: 1).

Truly, all must be done with the right motive. Our main aim should always be to give God the glory (Psalm 115: 1; Acts 12: 21–23; and 1 Corinthians 10: 31).

Spirit, Soul, and Body

Music is the only medium that blesses both man and God at the same time. To see it as an entertainment factor within our worship services is a gross misunderstanding of its purpose. Music is made up of three elements: melody, harmony, and rhythm. Mankind is also made up of three parts: spirit, soul, and body (1 Thessalonians 5: 23). It can be argued that music and the triune, or trichotomy, of mankind are intrinsically linked (i.e., the melody is likened to the spirit, harmony to the soul, and rhythm to the body).

Let's look at the link between music and the triune man more closely.

1. **Spirit and Melody**

The word of God enables us to know God and be conscious of Him (Hebrews 4: 12). The Bible explains that God is a Spirit: 'God is Spirit, and those who worship Him must worship in spirit and truth.' (John 4: 24).

To connect with God, it must be through the spirit, just as in order to know a tune of a song, it must be through its melody. It's almost impossible to recognise a tune without melody. In fact, whilst lecturing on this very subject at a Bible institute and seminary, I did a little experiment. I played a well-known tune just using one note. Not surprisingly, none of the students recognised the tune until I began to play the tune again with its melody. At that point, everyone knew the song. This is the importance of melody!

I believe that as we sing a song, the melody affects and connects to the spirit of mankind as it is the leading tune of a musical composition and delves deep in to the heart of a person when it is heard.

2. **Soul and Harmony**

Genesis 2: 7 states that man was created as a living soul. The soul consists of the mind, which includes the conscious, the will, and the emotions. The soul and spirit are mysteriously tied together and make up what the scriptures calls the heart. It is from the heart (soul) that we are called to love and worship God: 'You shall love the LORD your God with all your heart, with all your soul, and with all your strength.' (Deuteronomy 6: 5).

Have you heard a gospel choir when it is all singing the melody in unison and then all of a sudden it breaks out into harmony? It gives many people goose bumps as the emotions are awakened. Have you heard a full orchestra playing? If its members were all to play the tune together, as beautiful as it may sound, the full effect would not be heard until some instruments break out in various harmonies to compliment the tune. When harmony comes together, in any situation, not just music, it makes one's soul happy!

3. Body and Rhythm

The body is the entire material or physical structure of a human being, the flesh and bone (1 Corinthians 6: 20 and Romans 12: 1).

Rhythm is a strong regular repeating pattern of movement or sound. This is often called the beat or the pulse of the music. It is said that rhythm affects the physical body. When the body hears a beat, it is instinctive that the body wants to move.

To give a further explanation of how melody, harmony, and rhythm affect the triune man, let us imagine a choir singing the traditional version of the song 'Amazing Grace'.

It may begin with a soloist singing the main tune of the song. This is called the melody. When the audience hears this melody, it will instinctively touch the inner man (the spirit). As the song is built up, the choir will bring harmony, which is usually entailed by adding alto, tenor, bass, and other musical instruments. This supports the soloist's voice. When this is heard, it will begin to evoke an emotion within the listener (the soul).

Finally, the rhythms of the song affect the listener, who will then begin to innately tap his foot, nod the head, or clap the hands in time to the music (the body). Furthermore, the listener may even raise his hands in reaction to what he has heard. So here we have an example of how melody, rhythm, and harmony affect the triune man.

Music affects the whole being of man: melody (spirit), harmony (soul), and rhythm (body). It is an integral part of how mankind worships his creator.

Chapter 10

Notation and Cantillation

The Te'amim

If you were to look at ancient Hebrew text, you would see special symbols below and above the Hebrew words. These are called ta'amei ha-mikra, commonly known as (and herein referred to as) te'amim. Te'amim, translated as taste, includes a variety of symbols that scholars claim are the musical notes of the Bible. One of the functions of the te'amim is to provide a melody for the cantillation (singing) of the scriptures.

Let's pause here a moment. Wouldn't it be amazing if we could actually find out what notes, scales, and melodies were sung in the times of the great biblical patriarchs? Even though it may seem like a long shot, I really believe it is worth investigating.

Throughout the ages, many people have shown great interest in discovering the music of the Bible to ascertain how it was used in biblical times in worship and what it would have sounded like. Scholars have attempted to do this by carrying out various forms of research and applying different types of methodology in order to reach some kind of conclusion. As the subject matter is of considerable depth, it takes a great deal of commitment to collate and substantiate these discoveries.

One such scholar is Suzanne Haïk-Vantoura a French organist, teacher, composer, and leading expert in the area of biblical music notation. She documented a differing viewpoint to Lockyer in her book, *The Music of the Bible Revealed* (1991). She believed she had discovered an ancient Hebrew musical notation system. It was during my studies and research of ancient biblical music at the Birmingham Conservatoire, Birmingham, England, that I actually discovered lots of scholars who shared Haïk-Vantoura's opinion. However, it was Haïk-Vantoura's methodology and findings that really intrigued me, leading me to investigate her claims further.

I will not be discussing this subject deeply, but I thought it would be useful to have a basic knowledge of how the te'amim came about and how it was used.

Under the leadership of Rabbi Ben Asher, the Massoretes' objective was to create a single text that unified the traditions in existence and documented them in a way that would guarantee their preservation in the future. They did this by taking the oral traditions passed down from Moses' time and prepared the writings for literary publication, which we now know as the Tanakh. The Masoretes were a group of Jewish scholars whose name comes from the Hebrew word 'masorah', which means to bind or to hand down. They were the first to use the te'amim symbols as musical notations.

It is said that one of the concerns of the Masoretes was that Jews were beginning to forget the Hebrew language, which consisted of the letters, te'amim, and vowel pointings (we will discuss this later on). Originally, ancient Hebrew had no vowel pointings and only consonants. When reading these texts, one had to supply all of the vowels from memory, based on oral tradition, meaning it was passed down from generation to generation. Especially for people who were not schooled in Hebrew writing, the vowel pointings can make a big difference. Shortly, we will be looking at the difference between te'amim markings and vowel pointings, as one can be easily mistaken for the other.

Firstly, remembering that Hebrew is read from right to left, let's look at the following Hebrew words and the translated meanings:

לחם = fight

לחם = bread

Can you spot the difference? I guess you have realised that there is no difference except for the words' meanings. However, let's look at these words again, adding in the vowel pointings underneath the Hebrew letters:

לְחַם = fight

לֶחֶם = bread

It is the vowel pointings that the Masoretes put into place to give the words context and meaning! The transliteration and its definition is as follows:

לְחַם = lacham (to fight, do battle, make war)

לֶחֶם = lechem (bread, food, grain)

This is why I always encourage any scholar of the Bible to invest in a credible Bible dictionary (Strong's Concordance is a good one).

The te'amim can be viewed only in the Hebrew text, which is always read from right to left. The Hebrew word usually consists of the following three elements:

1. The Hebrew letters forming the words.

2. Vowel pointings.

3. Te'amim signs, also known as cantillation markings.

Having said all of this, unfortunately, the Masoretes did not supply instructions for interpreting these markings. Scholars agree that these markings at least serve to divide the text into sections and aid in the correct interpretation of the text. Scholars do believe they are cantillation markings, but the markings differ in meaning from person to person and across geographical regions.

However, Haïk-Vantoura has her own theory on the te'amim. In her findings, there is reference to the sublinear and superlinear te'amim. The sublinear te'amim are the te'amim markings found under the Hebrew text, and the superlinear te'amim are the te'amim markings found above the Hebrew text. These are not to be mistaken for the vowel pointings, which are a different set of symbols. This may take a little bit of study to differentiate the difference between the vowel markings and the te'amim. We will look into this later on in this chapter.

There is an interaction between the sublinear te'amim, which is a sign under the Hebrew word, and the superlinear te'amim, which is a sign above the Hebrew word. There is a fixed pitch for the sublinear te'amim in comparison to the superlinear te'amim, which has a relative pitch. This relative pitch is derived from the preceding sublinear te'amim.

For example, if the sublinear pitch, which will be fixed to one of eight notes, indicates to sing the note E over the word 'tabernacle', which has four syllables, the singer would sing the note E for each syllable. However, if the superlinear gives the sign over the final syllable of the word, the singer would then change to whatever pitch the superlinear sign is indicating. The superlinear pitch could also be decorated.

This might sound a bit complicated, but in modern-day terms, it can be compared to when a singer follows a score and sees various musical expressions (for example, sing lively, staccato, allegro, trill). However, with a superlinear te'amim, it is not an expression. Rather, it is a pitch.

There are two main modes that Haik-Vantoura has discovered in her research: the Psalmodic and the Prosodic. The Psalmodic mode is used mainly in the books of Psalms, Proverbs, and Job, while the Prosodic mode is mainly used in the rest of the Old Testament.

For the purpose of the following example, I will be concentrating on the Prosodic mode. The example we will look at is Exodus 10: 4: 'Or else, if you refuse to let My people go, behold, tomorrow I will bring locusts into your territory.'

This is seen in the Hebrew text as:

כִּי אִם־מָאֵן אַתָּה לְשַׁלֵּחַ אֶת־עַמִּי הִנְנִי מֵבִיא מָחָר אַרְבֶּה בִּגְבֻלֶךָ:

So let's break down this verse in accordance to the three elements:

i) The Hebrew words

כי אם־מאן אתה לשלח את־עמי הנני מביא מחר ארבה בגבלך:

ii) Vowel pointings

כִּי אִם־מָאֵן אַתָּה לְשַׁלֵּחַ אֶת־עַמִּי הִנְנִי מֵבִיא מָחָר אַרְבֶּה בִּגְבֻלֶךָ:

iii) Te'amim

כִּי אם־מאן אתה לשלח את־עָמִי הִנְנִי מביא מחר ארבה בגבלך:

Here is the Prosodic mode with G natural and the te'amim symbols and their names:

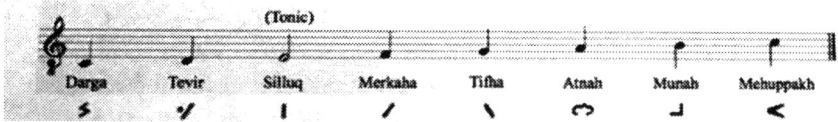

Please note that in the Prosodic mode, the tonic note is an E and does not start, as you would expect, on the C. So with this in mind, Haïk-Vantoura mentions that the third degree (Tifha) can very well be raised from the note G natural to a G sharp. If a G natural is used, this becomes the Phrygian mode. If a G sharp is used, this becomes the Phrygian Dominant mode.

Let's take a look at a breakdown of Exodus 10: 4 in the table below.

Hebrew word and Te'amim markings	Transliteration	English	Sub-linear	Super-linear	Haïk-Vantoura Note/pitch
כִּי	kî	Else	𝄥		D
אִם־מָאֵן	mā-'ên	refuse	╱		F
אַתָּה	'at-tāh	you	╲		G or G#
לְשַׁלֵּחַ	lə-šal-lê-aḥ	to let go	⌐		B
אֶת־עַמִּי	'am-mî	my people	⌢		A
הִנְנִי	hin-nî	behold		╲	B
מֵבִיא	mê-bî	I will bring	╱		F
מָחָר	mā-ḥār	tomorrow	𝄥		D
אַרְבֶּה	'ar-beh	the locusts	╲		G or G#
בִּגְבֻלֶךָ:	big-bu-le-ḳā.	into your territory			E

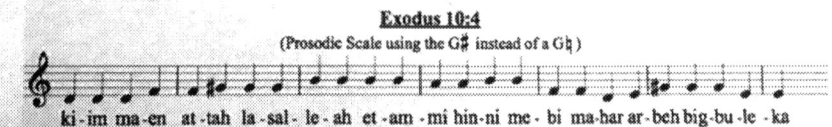

Exodus 10:4

(Prosodic Scale using the G♯ instead of a G♮)

ki - im ma -en at -tah la -sal - le - ah et -am -mi hin-ni me - bi ma-har ar -beh big -bu -le - ka

This is a score version of the above with the transliteration.

As you can see from the te'amim, according to Haik-Vantoura's deciphering, the first te'amim marking is D. The singer will continue to sing the note D on every syllable of each word until the next te'amim marking appears.

Please observe that the mode used here is the Phrygian Dominant mode. I have discovered that one of the common Jewish modes used today is the Phrygian Dominant mode, which is also known as the Ahavah Rabbah mode. Incidentally, one of the most traditional Jewish songs, 'Havah Nagilah', uses the Ahavah Rabbah mode. This mode consists of the notes E-F-G#-A-B-C-D-E.

Also using the same mode is a prayer and blessing recited daily, which is also called the Ahavah Rabbah prayer. The words 'Ahavah Rabbah' mean great love, and it is a blessing said to express the thanks of the people to God, the creator, for the great love He has shown to us. It is sung in the morning service before the Shema (Deuteronomy 6: 4–9).

Whilst praying, the four corners of the tzitzit are gathered as God is asked to bring peace to the four corners of the earth. The tzitzit are knotted fringes found on the prayer shawl, worn in Israel in ancient times and today. These knots were spaced in a certain way that add up to thirty-nine coils. This is the same numerical value as the name 'Hashem Echad', meaning God is One.

Singing

Throughout history, mankind has been singing. This is something that is inherent; it is a part of us. We like putting melody to words. Have you ever noticed that when you sing, you find it easy to remember words? We can retain thousands of words once a melody is added. In fact, researchers say that the brain remembers words better when they are contained in a catchy tune. Think of the many songs you have heard and known. If you were to do a tally, it may very well surprise you how many songs you actually know the words to. Our brains can store hundreds, and if we put our mind to it literally thousands, of songs in our memory, ready to be retrieved at an instant. Music and singing has a formidable mnemonic ability that neuroscientists are just beginning to fathom. They are discovering that our minds are hardwired to acknowledge, sort, and recall patterns in music and singing much better than we remember patterns in just words.

But of course, God knew from the beginning that singing would help retain words. After all, He created the brain. The custom of singing God's word is highly likely to have dated as far back as to the time of Moses. In Deuteronomy 31: 19–22, God speaks to Moses and orders him to teach Israel a song so that they would not forget God. So we could say that singing today helps remind us of what God has done for us through His Son, Jesus.

> Now therefore, write down this song for yourselves, and teach it to the children of Israel; put it in their mouths, that this song may be a witness for Me against the children of Israel. When I have brought them to the land flowing with milk and honey, of which I swore to their fathers, and they have eaten and filled themselves and grown fat, then they will turn to other

gods and serve them; and they will provoke Me and
break My covenant. Then it shall be, when many evils
and troubles have come upon them, that this song
will testify against them as a witness; for it will not
be forgotten in the mouths of their descendants, for
I know the inclination of their behaviour today, even
before I have brought them to the land of which I
swore to give them." Therefore Moses wrote this song
the same day, and taught it to the children of Israel.
(Deuteronomy 31: 19–22)

There are many other references in the Bible to singing,
suggesting that singing the scriptures was a common practice. The
Bible encourages us to sing many times in different situations and
gives us an example of how people sang in good times and in bad
times (Acts 16: 25–34, Luke 1: 46–55, Exodus 15: 1–21, 2 Chronicles
20: 21–22, 1 Samuel 18: 6–7, and 2 Samuel 22). However, nothing
gripped me more than when I read that Jesus sang. It can be easily
overlooked. It tells us in Matthew 26: 30: 'And when they had sung
a hymn, they went out to the Mount of Olives.'

When the Bible says 'they', it is referring to Jesus and His disciples.
This was the time after they had taken part in the Lord's Supper. But
what amazes me is that Jesus knew that not long from then, He would
be betrayed, arrested, tried by Annas, tried by Caiaphas, tried by the
Sanhedrin, tried by Pilate, tried by Herod, and then tried by Pilate
again. In addition, He was beaten and spat at. A crown of thorns
was placed on His head, and He would endure a very cruel death by
crucifixion. Yet, our Saviour sang.

When I think that Jesus knew what He was going to bare, even to the point of His sweat becoming as blood in the Garden of Gethsemane, and yet He still sang, I am humbled and left in awe.

It is well acknowledged that the Last Supper was the Passover meal (Exodus 12: 1–30) and that the Jewish Passover liturgy included special hymns drawn from the book of Psalms (these were actually songs). These hymns were known as the Hallel, meaning praise, and consisted of Psalm 113 through 118.

That's not the only time that we read that Jesus sang. The Bible tells us that Jesus sang in the midst of the congregation (Hebrews 2: 9–12). Also, in Zephaniah 3: 17, it says God will rejoice over you with singing.

Using Lyrics for God's Glory

The philosopher Aristotle said 'give me a child until he is 7 and I will show you the man.' Using the same theory, I believe that if you give me the words to the songs that a church sings, I will show you what that church believes. It is true that what we sing is what we normally adopt, so it is important that the songs we sing are biblically correct. The words of a Christian song should always take precedence over the music.

Take a look at these scriptures: Colossians 1: 15–20, Philippians 2: 5–11, and 1 Timothy 3: 16. Some Bible scholars believe that these verses were possibly early New Testament hymns or chants. If they were, notice that the words are Christ-centred. Don't get me wrong – there is a place for professionalism where music is concerned. In fact, I would robustly encourage all musicians to spend time in perfecting their instrument, and given the opportunity, to play skilfully to the

125

best of their ability. But we must always remember that it is the lyrics that carry the message. No matter how skilfully a musician may play their instrument, the instrument cannot physically say, 'Jesus is Lord.' However, if one sings 'Jesus is Lord!' accompanied with the music, the message is clear (Romans 10: 17).

Still on the point of words, during any given service, whilst we worship in song, do not feel surprised if the words are repeated. Some people may find this repetition boring or unnecessary. However, I do not believe there is anything wrong with this as long as the repetition is done to glorify the Lord. When we look at the book of Psalms, we see there is much repetition of certain phrases. For example, in Psalm 136, it repeats the words 'give thanks' and 'for His mercy endureth forever'. In Psalm 150, it says repeatedly 'praise ye the Lord' and 'praise Him'. Repetition is the mother of learning, and learning leads to understanding. After all, even in heaven the four beasts worshipped without resting, saying, 'holy, holy, holy is the Lord God Almighty, who was and is and is to come!' (Revelation 4: 8).

Imagine a preacher in the middle of a sermon quoting lyrics from a secular song or poem. Well, Paul did exactly that. He quoted from two philosophical writers, Epimenides and Aratus, and it is recorded in Acts 17: 28. I will not go into the finer details of this occasion, but it reads, 'for in Him we live and move and have our being, as also some of your own poets have said, 'For we are also His offspring.' (Acts 17: 28)

So let's take a closer look at this verse. Epimenides wrote the poem 'Cretica', and this is where the first part of verse 28 comes from. 'For in him we live, and move, and have our being;'

The second part Paul quoted was from the Cilician Stoic philosopher Aratus and was a part of a hymn to Zeus written in approximately 300 BC. 'For we are also his offspring.' (Acts 17: 28)

Let me make this clear. Both of these philosophers attributed their writings to Zeus. Actually, it is interesting to note here that the word 'philosophy' is made up of two Greek words: 'philein', which means to love, and 'sophia', which means wisdom. We can say that a basic interpretation of philosophy is the love of wisdom. There is nothing wrong with loving wisdom. In fact, Paul says in Ephesians 1: 17, 'that the God of our Lord Jesus Christ, the Father of glory, may give to you the spirit of wisdom and revelation in the knowledge of Him.'

James 1: 5 states, 'If any of you lack wisdom, let him ask of God ....' We are also encouraged about wisdom in Proverbs 14: 1. To acquire wisdom is accepted in the Bible. However, the Bible also makes it clear that the foundation and truth of the wisdom we seek must come through Christ.

So the question can be asked why Paul took lines from these poets and uses it in the middle of his sermon.

Paul was using Greek philosophy to reveal Jesus Christ and not to validate their philosophies about other gods. First of all, we need to acknowledge that all gifts and talents come from God. However, unfortunately, some people misdirect their gifts and talents and do not bring glory to the true God, Yahweh. As such, whatever your gift or talent may be, it must be used to bring glory to God.

To reiterate, Paul did not use the teachings or poems of the Greek philosophers to condone what they were saying, but he used it to reveal the truth of Christ. This can be clearly understood in Acts 17: 29–31.

> Therefore, since we are the offspring of God, we ought not to think that the Divine Nature is like gold or silver or stone, something shaped by art and man's devising. Truly, these times of ignorance God overlooked, but now commands all men everywhere to repent, because He has appointed a day on which He will judge the world in righteousness by the Man whom He has ordained. He has given assurance of this to all by raising Him from the dead.

Paul makes it clear that he was talking about Jesus Christ, who rose from the dead, and not Zeus!

As a musician myself, there are songs with certain lyrics I will not play. I can give you an example. I was playing in a recording studio, recording keyboards for a group, and one of their lyrics was using profanities against Christ and His name. So I refused to record for them, as their lyrics made it clear what their beliefs on Christ were, and they were against what I believed. If I had used my God-given gifts to record these profanities, I believe I would have been using my gifts to doing something that did not glorify God (1 Corinthians 10: 31).

I believe it is down to the individual person to know when to draw the line when it comes to music ministry on a whole. Suffice it to say, if the lyrics were neutral, I most likely would have played and recorded the song and at the same time using my talents as a witness of Christ. In my opinion, in all that we do, whether it be composing songs, choosing lyrics, contemplating whether to play for a nonsecular artist, or any other decision, we need to make concerning our gifts and talents. We must always seek God's guidance and His discernment. God sent His Spirit to guide us into all truth, and it is He who knows the mind and thoughts of God.

> 'And whatever you do in word or deed, do all in the name of the Lord Jesus, giving thanks to God the Father through Him.' (Colossians 3: 17)

Chironomy

It is believed that chironomy in the Old Testament was used to indicate the pitch and specific notes that the singers should sing by following the te'amim. Chironomy used hand and finger gestures to visually instruct the correct musical rendering of the Hebrew text. Haïk-Vantoura's findings led her to believe that chironomy was used in the Bible and is indirectly mentioned in scripture and is the root of the te'amim symbols. One of the scriptures where it is said to indicate chironomy is 1 Chronicles 25: 6–7.

> All these were under the direction of their father for the music in the house of the LORD, with cymbals, stringed instruments, and harps, for the service of the house of God. Asaph, Jeduthun, and Heman were under the authority of the king. So the number of them, with their brethren who were instructed in the songs of the LORD, all who were skillful, was two hundred and eighty-eight.

The word 'direction' in verse 6 (note in some versions is 'hands') is seen in relation to music that this could well be the use of chironomy, With this in mind, in the verse above, 'under the direction of' refers to the art of chironomy. This is likened to what a modern-day choir conductor would do.

Chironomy has survived in the Israeli tradition from Jewish ancient times to the present day.

In modern-day Church terms it could be argued that a type of chironomy is used by the choir director and enhances worship. It is a choir director's duty to not only lead the singers but to help the singers to interpret the melody and structure of a song. For example, if the words to a song say, 'You whisper to my soul', it is expected that the choir would sing this softly rather than at full volume. It is the choir director's duty to use his or her hands to indicate that the choir follow this instruction. The same can be said of the music director or worship leader who uses various signs to direct the musicians to interpret a song in order to draw the congregation closer to God in worship.

Modern-day conducting is mainly used to draw out the dynamics and tempo of the song. The legacy of chironomy, although in a slightly different format, is still used in modern worship.

This being the case, it shows that there were levels of hierarchy in the Bible, at the least where music was concerned.

So what relevancy does te'amim and chironomy have for you today? According to Marsha Bryan Edelman, a professor of music and education at Gratz College, the practice of te'amim and chironomy goes back to the time of Ezra when he stood and read portions of the Law to the Jewish people after their return from Babylonian exile (Nehemiah 8: 1–6). Edelman comments that he did not read the scriptures as is done today. Rather, he chanted them in order for the people to understand and to preserve its content. Preserving text is a normal occurrence throughout scripture (Jeremiah 30: 2; Habakkuk 2: 2; and Revelation 1: 1–2). In order to preserve your music for future generations, I would encourage you to preserve your songs by having them professionally scored or recorded. In properly documenting the lyrics, music, and musical notation of your song, it will ensure that if someone were to pick it up 100 years from now, he would sing and play it exactly as how you had intended.

Musical Terms in the Old Testament

Today, when we see a piece of scored music, we will notice that at the beginning of the score, and indeed throughout, we will often find information about that piece of music. Information such as the tempo, the key signature, the time signature, the instruments that should accompany the song, the composer, and the expression of how the music should be sang or played. However, one of the most important things is the title of the piece. Above the majority of the Psalms there are titles.

These titles are actually musical indications of how to express the song when played or sang. They are not translated, but they are transliterated from Hebrew. There are some Psalms where additional to the musical indication, the Psalmist gives further insight into the background to the Psalm. For example, in the title of Psalm 56, it explains the background to this Psalm is when the Philistines took him in Gath. The word Jonath-elemrechokim in the title means the silent dove of far-off places. Could it be that David actually felt like a dove carried off to far places?

Another example is in Psalm 60. In the title, it is explained that the background to the Psalm is the story of when David fought Aram-Naharaim and Aram-Zobah and then Joab returned to kill 12,000 Edomites in the Valley of Salt. It is interesting here that the instruction given is that this michtam, a poem and is to be taught as a memorial. This suggests that the musical inclination Shushan-eduth, which actually means testimony or witness, was aptly used.

Aijeleth Shahar is split into two words: aijeleth meaning hind, and shahar meaning dawn. Hence, the whole word means on the hind of the dawn. Some say it was the melody to which the psalm was sung. This is found in Psalm 22: 1.

Alamoth means young women or soprano. It is found in 1 Chronicles 15: 20 and in the title of Psalm 46: 1.

Al-taschith means do not destroy, a command to the chief musician or a title of a melody. It is found in the titles of Psalms 57, 58, 59, and 75.

Gittith means a wine press. It is commonly understood to be a stringed musical instrument from Gath (a city of the Philistines). Interestingly, David was a hiding from King Saul in Gath (1 Samuel 27: 1–7; 2 Samuel 15: 18). Scholars say that David learned to play one of the instruments from Gath at the time. Could it be that whilst David was in Gath, he actually made the gittith and then attributed Psalms 8, 81, and 84 to be played on this? This is not unusual, as David was known for making new instruments for praise unto God (2 Chronicles 7: 6).

Jonath-elemrechokim means the silent dove of far-off places and is probably the name of a melody. It is found in the title of Psalm 56.

Leannoth this means to afflict, oppress, humble, and be bowed down. It is found once in the Bible as Mahalath Leannoth, and together, the phrase means to humble or afflict. Finally, it is said that the mahalath is a guitar and that leannoth refers to the character of the psalm. It is found solely in the title of Psalm 88.

Mahalath means sickness, a company of dancers, or a harp. Mahalath could also be the name of a melody. It is found in the title of Psalm 53 and Psalm 88.

Maschil means a song or poem of contemplation or a deep reflective thought. Found in the title of Psalms 32, 42, 44, 45, 52, 53, 54, 55, 74, 78, 88, 89, and 142.

Michtam is a written poem found in the titles of Psalms 16, 56, 57, 58, 59, and 60.

Muthlabbean has no clear meaning; however, some have said it means on the death of Labben (an unknown person) or on the death of the son, meaning King David's son Absalom (2 Samuel 18: 33). Finally some believe it may mean it is the name of a musical instrument, or the name of an air to which the psalm was sung. Found in Ps. 9:1, and Ps. 48:14.

Nehiloth derived from a root word meaning to bore or perforate and therefore denotes perforated wind instruments of all kinds. It only appears in the title of Psalm 5.

Neginah means music, song, or taunt song and is a stringed instrument. Neginah comes from the root word negan, which means to play, strike strings, or to play a stringed instrument. It is found in the title of Psalm 61.

Neginoth was probably a stringed instrument or a poem set to music. It denotes all kinds of stringed instruments, such as the harp, psaltery, and the viol. It is found in the titles of Psalm 4, 6, 54, 55, 67, and 76.

Sheminith again has no clear meaning, but some have said it means eight, the eighth, and octave. It is either an eight-string instrument or even a musical term, supposed to denote the lowest note sung by men's voices (1 Chronicles 15: 21; Psalms 6 and 12).

Shigionoth derives from the verb shagah, meaning to reel about through drink. It occurs in the title of Psalm 7. Could this possibly mean that this psalm was written under strong emotions?

Shoshannim means lilies, or it could refer to the fact that it is a musical instrument that resembled a lily (a trumpet). It is found in the title of Psalms 45 and 69.

Shushaneduth/Shoshannimeduth is split into two words, shushan/shoshan, meaning lily and eduth meaning testimony or witness. It has been said that, in its entirety, the word could be the title of a song. It is found in the title of Psalms 60 and 80.

Song of degrees means what comes up, thoughts, step, stair, and ascent. It is specifically a climatic progression. It is found in the titles of Psalms 120 to 134.

Chapter 11

The Colour and Sound of Praise and Worship

The Colour of Praise and Worship

Maybe you have never thought of this concept before, but when we are praising and worshipping God, we are giving homage to a God who loves colour.

Firstly, it is important to say that there are laws governing the world of colour. Colour plays a huge part in our everyday life. If you stop reading right now and just look around, you will see that there is colour everywhere! Is this something that you have taken for granted?

Did you know that colour is primarily activated by light? A white light is composed of various colours. I would not profess to be an expert in this area, but it is said that all light travels at the same speed through a vacuum, but each colour has a different wavelength and frequency. Before I go on to share with you what their different wavelength and frequencies are, let me give you a definition of these words.

Wavelengths are measured in nanometres, abbreviated as nm, which is a unit of spatial measurement that is one thousand-millionth, or one billionth, of a metre. The frequency of a wave, abbreviated as THz, is determined by the total number of complete waves or wavelengths, that pass a given point each second.

There are seven colours in the spectrum (red, orange, yellow, green, blue, indigo, and violet), and each one has its own approximate frequency and wavelength. They are as follows:

Red: frequency 435–495THz, wavelength 685–605nm

Orange: frequency 495–515THz, wavelength 605–585nm

Yellow: frequency 515–535THz, wavelength 585–560nm

Green: frequency 535–630THz, wavelength 560–475nm

Blue: frequency 630–660THZ, wavelength 475–455nm

Indigo: frequency 660–680THz, wavelength 455–440nm

Violet: frequency 680–740THz, wavelength 440–405nm

If we remove light from an object, our vision of the colour of the object will be largely diminished. This is because the visible spectrum (wavelength 390–750nm and frequency 400–790THz) is a subset of the electromagnetic spectrum that is visible to the human eye.

When we look at the grass and we say it is green, we only know this due to the retinas in our eyes that have unique cells called cones. When we look at an object, let's say, a banana, and the light hits the object, part of the light is absorbed. The remainder of it is reflected. The wavelengths that are absorbed or reflected depend on the substance of the object. For example, a ripe banana reflects wavelengths of approximately 570–580nm. The brain recognises these as the wavelengths in the range of yellow light, and subsequently, we see it as a ripe yellow banana.

To explain a little further, amazingly, the human eye has approximately 6 to 7 million cones. The cones respond differently to different coloured lights, with the highest response being to red light, approximately one third being to green and the least to blue. The changing degrees of these lights cause them to react when they are hit by the light from the banana. This causes a process to take place along the nerve from our eyes to our brain which then enables us to see the colour yellow. The whole process takes a fraction of a second. Wow! We are truly wonderfully made (Psalm 139: 14).

Having now looked at the science, the question you may ask is how does this all relate to praise and worship? Colour features prominently in the Bible, but it would be an error to ascribe some kind of spiritual or mystical message to the colours. However, there are some clear patterns and verses that arise that show us a clear symbolism attached to the colours in the Bible. For instance, in Exodus 39: 2, there is a list of colours relating to the design of the priest's ephod, mentioned twenty-four times throughout the Bible, and every time they are mentioned, it is in the exact same order. These colours are gold, blue, purple, and scarlet. Gold symbolises the divinity of God, His righteousness, and the glory of Christ; blue symbolises heaven; purple was the colour associated with Yahweh and the colour worn by Kings symbolising royalty; and scarlet symbolises a picture of Christ, His atoning power, and represents life.

Yet, if you keep at the forefront of your mind that it is light that has all colours within it, you will begin to see a deeper revelation to the declaration of Jesus that He is the light of the world (John 8: 12). I would suggest that all the colours of the spectrum dwelt within

Jesus! So having saying that, let's delve deeper into the multicoloured nature of God.

There are multifaceted colours of God's wisdom. Nothing exists outside of God's knowledge because He is omniscient. Ephesians 3: 10 says, 'to the intent that now the manifold wisdom of God might be made known by the church to the principalities and powers in the heavenly places.'

The word 'manifold' here is the Greek word 'polypoikilos', which means marked with great variety of colours. I believe the Bible is saying that God's wisdom is multifaceted, dare I say multicoloured! He has every colour and more to His wisdom than we will ever understand.

There are multifaceted colours of miracles and gifts of the Holy Spirit. There is no miracle or gift that God cannot provide for you. Hebrews 2: 4 it says, 'God also bearing witness both with signs and wonders, with various miracles, and gifts of the Holy Spirit, according to His own will?' The word 'various' is the Greek word 'poikilos', which means various colours. I believe the Bible is saying that there is no sickness that God cannot heal due to His multifaceted nature.

There are multifaceted colours of God's grace. 1 Peter 4: 10 says, 'As each one has received a gift, minister it to one another, as good stewards of the manifold grace of God.' Again, the word 'manifold' here is the Greek word 'poikilos' – as explained above, it means various colours. Hence, I believe the Bible is highlighting to us that God's grace is far able to exceed our wildest imaginations.

However, on the reverse, Satan pretends to have light. Paul says in 2 Corinthians 11: 14 that the devil transforms himself as an angel of light. The word transforms is from a Greek word, which means to hide behind or disguise. So Satan, the father of lies (John 8: 44), pretends to be something he is not.

As such, everything that Satan does is a lie. Even though there are diverse colours of disease (Matthew 4: 24), sickness (Mark 1: 34), temptation (1 Peter 1: 6), and lust (Titus 3: 3), from a natural point of view, colour cannot be seen if there is no light. As such, the colours that the devil has are actually ineffective and false.

Thus, when we return to the subject of praise and worship, we remember that, as mentioned, Jesus is the light of the world. He has various colours of Himself to offer us. There's a colour for every need. No wonder in the tabernacle of Moses and the temple of Solomon colour is of great importance. Furthermore, in the book of Revelation, God's Temple was decorated with colours. Could this be another sign of what God is trying to communicate to us? I think so, especially as we reflect on Paul's statement that we now are the temple of God (1 Corinthians 3: 16).

Calling out to every believer of Yahweh, Jesus also says you are the light of the world (Matthew 5: 14–16).

The Sound of Praise and Worship

Have you ever thought of the things that are around you that you have never seen? This may sound ridiculous, but there are important things that exist that we do not see. One such thing is vibrations.

There are two main properties of a regular vibration — the amplitude and the frequency — that affect the way it sounds.

Amplitude is the size of the vibration, and this determines how loud the sound is. Larger vibrations make a louder sound.

Frequency is measured in Hertz and is abbreviated as Hz. It is the speed of the vibration, and this determines the pitch of the sound. It is significant in music where there is a strong regular waveform. A4 is commonly tuned to 440Hz, thus having every instrument tuned to this frequency.

Every sound that we hear derives from a vibration. Musical notes are ultimately vibrations and every note can be set to its own frequency. There are many ways to produce sound, but sound cannot be produced without vibrations. So every sound that we hear derives from a vibration. These vibrations then create sound waves that move through mediums such as air and water before reaching our ears. Once it comes to our ears, it becomes sound, and our brain deciphers it so we can respond to what we hear.

There are two different aspects to sound. There's a physical process that produces sound energy to start with and sends it shooting through the air, and there's a separate psychosomatic process that happens as we hear the vibrations of the sound, which converts the incoming sound energy into sensations that we deduce as noises, speech, and music.

In fact, science now agrees that everything sends off some type of wave. Typically, whenever people think of wave they may first think about an ocean or even the wave of a hand. However, did you know that right now as you are reading this book that there are waves all around with radio waves, microwaves, sound waves, sun beams, and colour too? God describes the vibrations of the stars, 'When the morning stars sang together, And all the sons of God shouted for joy?' (Job 38: 7) The word 'sang' in this scripture refers to the Hebrew verb 'ranan', meaning to vibrate the voice, shout for joy, praise, and exultation.

Furthermore, Jeremiah 51: 48 says, 'Then the heavens and the earth and all that is in them Shall sing joyously over Babylon; For the plunderers shall come to her from the north," says the LORD.' The word 'sing' in this verse refers to ranan, and it is amazing to read that everything will vibrate. There are many other examples throughout scripture where ranan is used concerning to show the heavens and earth send out vibrations of praise.

In Genesis, God spoke creation into being, and it suggests that vibration originated from God. This serves to prove right what Paul said to the Colossians,

> For by Him all things were created that are in heaven and that are on earth, visible and invisible, whether thrones or dominions or principalities or powers. All things were created through Him and for Him. (Colossians 1: 16)

Not only did His word bring creation into existence, but His word held creation together as stated in Colossians 1: 17, 'And He is before all things, and in Him all things consist.' The Greek word for 'consist' is synistēmi, which means to place together, to bring together, or to band together. All matter including its particles such as electrons, protons, and neutrons, which are particles that form atoms, are held together by the very words that originate from God's mouth.

The words that God speaks live forever and supersede our material reality. 'Heaven and earth will pass away, but My words will by no means pass away.' (Luke 21: 33). In fact, it is Christ, who is the word that form creation as He is the creator.

> In the beginning was the Word, and the Word was
> with God, and the Word was God. And the Word
> became flesh and dwelt among us, and we beheld His
> glory, the glory as of the only begotten of the Father,
> full of grace and truth. (John 1: 1, 14)

I will not look into quantum mechanics now; I will leave that for the experts. However, from scripture, we see that God's words shape physical matter, but the words themselves are a greater reality than what they create because they "never pass away." Furthermore, the Bible says that God upholds all things by the power of His words (Hebrews 1: 3).

It is important to acknowledge that we self-regulate what we say as these words once released cannot be taken back.

If we use our words in a negative way towards people or ourselves, we are in actual fact releasing negative vibrations that affect the body. Have you ever been around music that is just not right, or have you heard something that makes you wince and want to leave the vicinity? Well, this is what is known as bad vibes.

Think about the teachings of Christ, He taught us to speak to a mountain, and it will be moved. When Christ brought people back from the dead, He spoke life. When He was healing people, He spoke life (Psalm 107: 20). Just as how there is a law that governs colour and gravity, I would suggest there is a law that governs words that we speak (Proverbs 18: 21). Hence, we must be careful of what we say and endeavour to speak life! What I mean by this is that we must not gossip, tell lies, or say negative things over ourselves.

I would encourage you to use words that are in line with the teachings of the word of God. The Bible says in Psalm 103: 20 that the angels of God will work on our behalf once they have heard the Word of God.

Negative words that release negative vibrations into the atmosphere open a gateway for Satan to work. Positive words that are in line with the teachings of the word of God release the power of God into our lives. 'For by your words you will be justified, and by your words you will be condemned' (Matthew 12: 37). So Jesus explains this in the physical. I believe this is the same in the spiritual.

So in praise and worship unto God, the sound that we should release must be coupled with the word of God.

Conclusion

To fully encapsulate the subject of music, praise, and worship in one book would be like trying to fit the world into a box – it is impossible!

Although I have discussed at length subjects such as the origins of music from a biblical perspective, the significance of praise and worship, the role of dance in worship, the difference between the tabernacle and the temple, singing, biblical music notation systems, and how colour and sound affect worship, my research in this subject matter of this book is an ongoing process. Just like Paul who desired for the Ephesians to have a greater understanding of God's love (Ephesians 3: 17–18), I have found that there are much deeper aspects of music, praise, and worship yet to be understood.

What I have learnt along this journey is that having the right motive, in whichever way we choose to express our worship to God, is the key!

When we reflect on the account of Jesus' visit to Martha and Mary's house (Luke 10: 38–42), we see that the sisters had the same motive – to worship and honour Christ – but their method and focus were completely different. Martha chose to honour Christ through the work of her hand (Luke 10: 40), whereas Mary chose to honour Him by sitting at His feet and taking in His every word (Luke 10:

39). Of the two, Jesus said Mary had 'But one thing is needed, and Mary has chosen that good part, which will not be taken away from her' (Luke 10: 42). Mary's method proved to be better as her focus was purely on Christ!

Now was Jesus advocating an abstinence from housework? If that were the case, I am sure that there would be a worldwide cheer! Sorry to burst your bubble, but I do not believe Jesus was saying this. I believe he was helping Martha to refocus on what was truly important – remember the works we do now and are seen by man will come to its end, but it is our worship, which is invisible to man but seen by God, that will remain eternal (2 Corinthians 4: 18).

A similar event happened when a woman interrupted a debate between Jesus and the Pharisees. She came in and fell at Jesus' feet crying; she then proceeded to wash His feet with her tears and dried them with her hair (Luke 7: 38). Simon criticised her act, but Jesus' reply that once again showed the right motivation coupled with the right focus is what pleases God. Her sins were forgiven because of her actions (Luke 7: 44–48).

Remember in all that we do, only what we do for God will last (1 Corinthians 15: 58). So I encourage you to make sure you have the right motive and the right focus. As Jesus said, God is looking for true worshippers who worship Him in spirit and in truth (John 4: 23–24).

I hope that in your venture to better understand the biblical theology behind music, praise, and worship that you keep this question at the forefront of your mind: What is my motive, and what is my focus? I truly believe if we could all ask ourselves this question, before we pick up a pen to compose a song or a microphone to sing or an instrument to play, then we would be one step closer to fully understanding what it is to fulfil our purpose of being a true worshipper of Yahweh.

Works Cited

Adam C. *Clarke's Commentary on the Bible*. Nashville: Thomas Nelson Incorporated, 1997.

Anderson, W., 2011, *Simmer Down: The Problem of Playing Too Skillfully*, Worship Leader Available at http://worshipleader.com/simmerdown/

Brown S, Merker B, Wallin NL. *The Origin of Music*. Cambridge, MA: Massachusetts Institute of Technology, 2000.

Burgh TW. 2006. *Listening to the Artifacts: Music Culture in Ancient Palestine*. London and New York: T & T Clark International, 2006.

Christensen-Dalsgaard J. 2004. *Music and the Origin Of Speeches*. JMM Vol 2, Section 2, 2004.

Combarieu J. 1930. *Histoire de la Musique*. Paris: Armand Colin, 1930.

Concise Oxford English Dictionary, ed 12. Oxford: OUP, 2011.

D'Errico F, Villa P, Pinto Lona AC, Ruiz Idarraga R. 'A Middle Palaeolithic origin of music? Using cave-bear bone accumulations to assess the Divje Babe I bone 'flute'. *Antiquity Publications* Vol 72, No. 275, p.65-79, 1998.

Edelman MB. *Discovering Jewish Music.* Philadelphia: The Jewish Publication Society, 2003.

Edelman, M., (date unknown), *Cantillation: Chanting, or Leyning, the Bible,* My Jewish Learning. Available at http://www.myjewishlearning.com/article/cantillation-chanting-the-bible/2/

Edleman, M. B. *Cantillation:Chanting, or Leyning, the Bible.* Available at: http://www.myjewishlearning.com/culture/2/Music/Synagogue_and_Religious_Music/Cantillation.shtml

Fletcher P. Illustration of a Timbrel/Tabret. 2016. fletch726@gmail.com

Haïk-Vantoura, S. (Paris, 1978) *La Musique de la Bible Révélée*; Translated by D. Weber (1991) as *The Music of the Bible Revealed.* Berkeley. BIBAL Press and King David's Harp Inc.

Haïk-Vantoura S. La Musique de la Bible Révélée - une notation millénaire décryptée. Paris: Lethielleux, 1998.

Hesk I. *Passport to Jewish Music: Its History, Traditions, and Culture.* California: Greenwood Publishing, 1994.

Hutchinson E. *Music of the Bible.* Boston: Gould and Lincoln, 1864.

Jacobson JR. *Chanting the Hebrew Bible.* Philadelphia: The Jewish Publication Society, 2005.

Kamien R. *Music: An Appreciation.* New York: McGraw-Hill, 2002.

Lancaster I. *Deconstructing the Bible, Abraham izn Ezra's Introduction to the Torah.* London: Routledge Curzon, 2003.

Levin S. 'The Traditional Chironomy of the Hebrew Scriptures'. *Journal of Biblical Literature* 87, p. 59-70, 1968.

Lockyer Jr H. *All the Music of the Bible.* Massachusetts: Hendrickson Publishers, 2004.

Lubbock Bart J. *The Pleasures of Life.* Philadelphia: Henry Altemus, 1894.

Machabey A. *La Musique des origins a nos jours.* Paris: Larousse, 1946.

McCorkle DF. *The Davidic Cipher: Unlocking the Hidden Music of the Psalms.* Colorado: Outskirts Press, 2009.

Nee W. *The Spiritual Man.* New York: Christian Fellowship Publishers, 1968.

Noll M. *We Are What We Sing.* PUB: Christianity Today, 12 July 1999: 37.

Packer, J. I. *The Plan of God* Available at: http://www.the-highway.com/plan_Packer.html

Randel D. *The New Harvard Dictionary of Music.* Cambridge, MA: The Belknap Press of Harvard University, 1986.

Richards L. *The Revell Bible Dictionary.* Ada, MI: Revell, 1994.

Richards, L. 1999, T*he Global Concise Bible Dictionary.* Carlisle: STL UK

Sacks O. *Musicophilia: Tales of Music and the Brain.* New York: Random House, 2007.

Schrader D., 2004, *Song Story: Matt Redman's "The Heart of Worship",* Crosswalk Online magazine. Available at http://www. crosswalk.com/church/worship/song-story-matt-redmans-the-heart-of-worship-1253122.html

Sherrane, R. *Music History 102: a Guide to Western Composers and their music* Available at: http://www.ipl.org/exhibit/mushist/rom/berlioz.htm

Strong J. *The New Strongs Exhaustive Concordance of the Bible.* Nashville, TN: Thomas Nelson Publishers, 1996.

Tozer AW. *Whatever Happened To Worship.* Camphill, PA: Christian Publications, 1986.

Vincent, J. 2013, *New Study Shows How Singing Synchronises Choirs' Heartbeat,* Available at http://www.independent.co.uk/news/science/new-study-shows-how-singing-synchronises-choirs-heartbeat-8698315.html

Wheeler, J. H. (2003) *The Hebrew Musical Accents (te'amim).* Available at http://www.bibal.net/04/musico/psalms-iii/pdf/wheeler_accents-a.pdf

Wheeler, John H. (2010) *Music of the Bible Revealed.* Available at http://www.rakkav.com/Biblemusic/index2.htm

Williamson GI. *The Westminster Shorter Catechism.* New Jersey: P&R Publishing Company, 2003.

Printed in the United States
By Bookmasters